What lawyers are

"Bob Weiss is an outstanding marketing consultant for lawyers. Using Bob's invaluable market insight and strategies this past year I obtained several new, high-value clients and increased the value of my billings by 25 percent from the previous year."

Thomas Cunningham, Nyemaster, Goode, West, Hansell & O'Brien, P.C.

"I attribute much of the success of my practice to the coaching I received from Bob as I moved from an associate to partner. He assisted with my identification of target clients formalized my review process for involvement in groups and community activities and assisted with my writing my marketing plan, which I revisit often. The foundation he helped me lay has created a great career path for me."

Karen Samuels Jones, Stinson Leonard Street, LLP.

"Bob is unquestionably one of the premier legal marketing and public relations professionals in the country. He possesses a keen knowledge of the legal industry and particularly the decision making processes of those who engage lawyers— consumers, business and other lawyers. His thinking is original and he tailors marketing plans to the specific needs and objectives of his clients. Moreover, he is 100 percent reliable and is able to respond to a time sensitive marketing opportunity and deliver an effective product within hours."

Dale Perdue, Clark, Perdue & List, Co, LPA.

"I have known Bob 26 years. Bob is an exceptional marketing consultant who really understands professional service firms and what it takes to help them be successful. He has a dynamic and focused approach to counseling and coaching clients to produce an increase to bottom line financial results. I actively promote Bob to my clients and wouldn't hesitate to endorse him to anyone who needs a "top notch" marketing professional."

Michael Smith, SBC & Associates, Inc.

"Bob knows his client and the market they are pursuing.
He is always prepared, creative and knowledgeable. He is the best
law firm marketer I have worked with in 25 years of practice."

Dan Patterson, Conflict Resolution Services, Inc.,
and former managing partner of Roberts Levin & Patterson, LLP.

"Bob is up to date on the trends in MY practice and also on
where I am and what I should be doing to improve. Every time we meet
he has excellent suggestions on how to improve my situation."

William Feemster, Touchstone Bernays.

"My firm has consulted with Bob on marketing matters
and has found him to have clear understanding of the unique issues
to deal with in marketing lawyers and their businesses.
Bob is enthusiastic and a pleasure to work with."

Tom Kearns, Fairfield and Woods, P.C.

"Bob Weiss is one of the most candid and
knowledgeable experts in marketing legal professionals.
I have seen him speak at meetings and with clients and you always
get straight-forward, honest information without all the sales fluff.
If you are serious about growing a legal practice and using
measurable metrics to gauge success, I recommend him."

Bill Fukui, President, Page 1 Solutions, LLC, a leading legal SEO provider.

"Bob is a highly creative, think out-of-the-box marketing consultant.
He is smart, a quick study and knows his subject well. Further,
he is trustworthy and reliable. I recommend him highly."

Dan Recht, Recht & Kornfeld, PC.

"Bob Weiss was onboard, as a business-marketing consultant,
with a law firm when I joined the firm as administrator.
I have served the legal industry for 28 years and dealt with
many business/marketing consultants. Bob was by far the best."

Richard Turnbow, Avera & Smith, LLP.

"Bob has become an invaluable asset to our firm. He has taught everyone in the firm, including staff, how to build productive networks, enhance existing client relations/production and improve individual image among peers in the legal community. Bob's approach is very simple but it works. If you are disciplined, Bob will work for you. Bob now sits in on major strategy and planning meetings with the partners as an integral member of our team. His experience and connections benefited our firm immensely. His understanding of how the press operates has kept lawyers out of PR trouble. I cannot recommend Bob more highly – he has been the perfect complement to our professional and financial performance."

John Zakhem, Jackson Kelly PLLC.

"Bob Weiss is an expert in law office marketing/client procurement. His knowledge greatly increased my client retention and new business development. Unfortunately, many lawyers make horrible business people. As such, if you desire more clients, I strongly encourage you to speak with Bob."

Jeffery Hyslip, Macey Aleman Hyslip & Searns.

"Bob's insight into what our firm needed to do to make marketing a part of all activities was very helpful. His work laid the foundation for a broad based awareness of business development and helped us create a plan and the method for following up and assigning responsibility. His experience with many firms allows him to provide examples of what works, and perhaps more importantly, what doesn't."

Roger Whitaker, Luper Neidenthal & Logan, LPA.

"Bob has been a tremendous help in developing my career. He understands that professional development is more than identifying potential clients. His advice has benefited me professionally and personally. I recommend Bob to anyone looking for a coach that will take the time to understand your unique situation and help overcome the obstacles in your way. His many years of experience have helped provide a much needed perspective in my career."

Erik Groves, The Law Office of Erik R. Groves.

"Bob did an excellent job of positioning our law firm
for expansion into new practice areas and helped increase revenue
through a strategic marketing program."

David Bradley, Walters Balido & Crain, LLP.

"Over the years, I have worked with Bob on many mutual clients.
I continue to be impressed by his intensity, intelligence and creativity.
He really understands what it takes to position a law firm as
a preeminent firm in the market. Every one of Bob's clients
is better off because of him. Bob gets it!"

Dan Goldstein, Page 1 Solutions,
founder of one of the country's leading legal website design and SEO companies.

"My law firm and I have been working with Bob for 15 years.
Bob is always ahead of the curve when it comes to advising us
regarding marketing our legal services namely, what the popular
literature is telling us to do today, Bob was having us do three years ago.
Moreover, Bob has always had the pulse of both the Colorado
and national legal markets which has resulted not only
in us having business opportunities but making connections
that ended up being lateral hires. Finally, Bob surrounds himself
with colleagues that are equally as talented as he.
This translates into timely advice and assistance."

Hal Bruno, Robinson Waters & O'Dorisio, PC.

"Bob really understands lawyers, and that's an incredible asset
because it's his goal to get us to stretch beyond our comfort zones
in the business development arena. He's a valuable partner
in dealing with the media, learning to use new media,
balancing traditional and evolving marketing strategies, and
building a marketing worldview so that this extremely important
function of lawyering is an achievable part of what we do every day.
Bob's professional advice is all about helping his clients
get results, and given the other demands of our day jobs,
isn't that what every one of us needs?"

Mark Grueskin, then of Heizer Paul Grueskin and now at Recht Kornfeld PC

Legal
Marketing
in Brief

Bob Weiss

Alyn·Weiss & Associates, Inc.®

DENVER

For information or to order additional copies, contact
Alyn-Weiss & Associates, Inc.
themarketinggurus.com

ISBN 978-0-998-11610-5

Book Design by
Scott Johnson

Fifth Edition, September 2016

Dedication

With thanks to those who have suggested topics,
edited my work and encouraged me over the years.

Tracey Blake

Amber Vincent

Shari Jacob

John Treddenick

Jessica Jaramillo

Jack Hanley

Table of Contents

Introduction:
"Tips, not tomes"

This book is a compilation of marketing tips and observations, nearly every one of which you can immediately apply to your firm or individual practice.

Many appeared in a monthly advice column, "Weiss' Monthly Marketing Brief," which I was asked to write, for a number of years, for *Law Practice Today*, the e-zine of the Law Practice Management Section of the American Bar Association. A number of these, I was told, were some of the most often read articles on the ABA's site. Others were cited as sources in presentations. I know that because amused clients in audiences texted me on a number of occasions. They said someone had just cited my stuff at a convention (at a resort where I wish I had been at the time).

Today, about 5,000 lawyers, legal marketers, firm administrators, and other professionals subscribe to "Weiss' Monthly Marketing Brief." (Go to www.themarketinggurus.com and you can too.) This widespread circulation, I suppose, is because I resolved to keep every article I wrote as short as possible. Tips, not tomes, have been my goal. Also, I often write about issues that my clients have recently confronted to ensure relevance.

Numerous original articles have been updated in this edition. This is due to changed market conditions, the advance of technology, new surveys and feedback from my readers. In advance, I apologize for some repetition and overlap from tip to tip—so much of what we do interrelated.

Don't hesitate to contact me directly with relevant data or about your (perhaps differing and better) views of these topics.

Bob Weiss
weiss@themarketinggurus.com
Denver, Colorado
August 2016

Lawyers and Marketers:
The Natural (Productive) Tension Between Them

❖

Surveys indicate attorneys have growing dissatisfaction with their internal and external law firm marketing providers. That frustration is equally in place among the ranks of law firm marketers.

This is true despite increased understanding of marketing on both sides and the successful implementation of increasingly sophisticated results-producing business development programs at firms both large and small.

What lawyers and their marketers should understand is that a natural tension will always exist between them.

Here's why:

- Lawyers tend to look over their shoulders because they are trained to rely on that which is tested, for precedent. Marketers look in the opposite direction, to that not yet done by competitors, seeking meaningful differentiation, to create a brand and obtain a promotional advantage.

- To become a law firm partner, a lawyer must be a successful project manager, whether handling disputes or transactions. Legal matters tend to move forward on a broad front with numerous tasks coming together near the end. Marketers handle complex project management, but must proceed more linearly, requiring approvals in a specific order; approvals subsequently modified require backtracking, in many cases forcing marketers to start the project anew. This can cause significant frustration, delay and budget busting.

- Law firms have multiple owners, flattening the decision hierarchy. Generally, no single lawyer has absolute authority to make a binding decision. Legal marketing providers, both outside consultancies and internal departments, have much clearer hierarchies. A single person often can make a big decision absent review.

- Marketers commonly struggle to understand the lawyer and law firm decision-making process. Marketers fail to understand lawyers offer no document or argument absent a teardown of all angles in advance in a comprehensive search of possible challenges. Marketers must understand the necessity of this; what's written binds, what is argued cannot be taken back.

These differences in thinking and approach, if recognized, respected, and dealt with constructively, can be successfully managed to everyone's profit.

Chapter 1:
What Really Drives Billing Rates?

— ◆ —

More than 90 percent of corporate legal departments are shifting their work to firms in smaller cities to control legal costs. In addition, 75 percent of timekeepers who asked for rate increases between 2007 and 2013 were able to get in-house counsel to approve them with the largest increases being for junior associates.

Those are a few of the many intriguing results from The 2013 Real Rate Report, billed as "the legal industry's only benchmarking report built with actual invoice data from corporations across industries." The study sells for $4,500. (We got a deal on that rather breathtaking price tag because we agreed to read it carefully, give its sponsors a bit of help with their marketing, blog about it and write this article.)

The report is a compilation of invoices for $7.6 billion of fees billed over 48 months. Those invoices came from more than 3,500 domestic law firms billing for nearly 34,500 partners, 47,500 associates, and in excess of 121,000 timekeepers overall. The analysis covered 24.9 million invoice line items and 27.9 million hours billed to 62 companies. Those companies represent a solid cross-section of domestic and international industrial and services firms including insurance carriers.

The information came directly from "data contained in CT TyMetrix's matter management and electronic billing data warehouse," making it unlike any other study of rates to date. CT's clients gave the company "explicit permission" to assemble and publish the data. The data was scrubbed to ensure anonymity of both the companies and law firms, all of which were aware of the project.

Founded in 1994, CT created the first task-based and first online e-billing system. They have 150+ clients, corporate and insurance, and work with 18,000+ "participating" law firms. The report's co-sponsor was the Corporate Executive Board, which was founded in 1983 and has a staff of 1,700 located around the world directly serving nearly 5,000 corporations, nonprofits, and government agencies with best practices, benchmarking datasets and analytical tools. Their goal was to stimulate "reflection and debate in companies and law firms." Those of us who work in and with law firms know there has hardly been a shortage of that following the Great Recession. Big firms worry incessantly about losing corporate and carrier work to smaller firms. The smaller firms have always tried to figure out why big companies won't hire them consistently despite huge rate differences and comparable, even superior, lawyer skill sets.

Why a second year in NYC bills more than an 18-year partner in Minneapolis?

The report reveals:

Statistical Model of Lawyer Rates

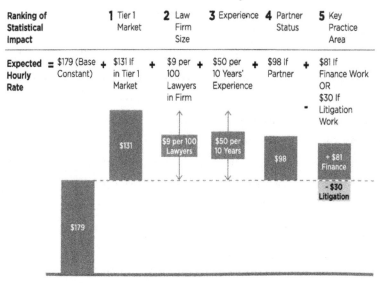

Ranking of Statistical Impact	1 Tier 1 Market	2 Law Firm Size	3 Experience	4 Partner Status	5 Key Practice Area
Expected Hourly Rate =	$179 (Base Constant) +	$131 If in Tier 1 Market +	$9 per 100 Lawyers in Firm +	$50 per 10 Years' Experience +	$98 If Partner +	$81 If Finance Work OR $30 If Litigation Work

n = 6,186 lawyers.

Lawyer B
Second-Year Associate

Base: $179

Tier 1 Market: +$131
(New York City)

1,000-Lawyer Firm: +$90

Two Years' Experience: +$10

Associate: +$0

Non-Key Practice
Area (M&A): +$0

Total: $410/Hour

Lawyer C
Partner

Base: $179

Non-Tier 1 Market: +$0
(Minneapolis)

300-Lawyer Firm: +$27

20 Years' Experience: +$100

Partner: +$98

Key Practice
Area (Litigation): -$30

Total: $374/Hour

"... in-house counsel may, in fact, be paying for access to a network of expertise and experience rather than the expertise and experience of the lawyer representing them."

Southern cities showed the biggest rate increases. That "may be correlated with the changing geography of corporate activity in United States and the recent shift of more corporate headquarters to the South," the report said, adding that rate increases follow the increased presence of multi-office firms in southern markets over the past 15 years.

Partnerships of local firms with lawyers of comparable or even superior capability to the multi-office lawyers across the street routinely howl about their comparatively depressed rates. What could corporate counsel be thinking? Comparisons are relatively easy to make, they say.

Maybe you're making the wrong pitch.

The report says "preliminary data" indicates the size of a firm is "associated with faster execution" and that "clients may be paying for speed of resolution." Those are marketing themes and benchmarks of which to take note. How much do you know about your speed of execution and time to resolution compared to your larger rivals? You probably know quite a bit if your larger rival used to be your local competitor and simply changed names (and rates) by merging with a regional or national firm.

Another take-away is the data reveals "a positive relationship between spending and rates" at a firm and that the result "is the opposite of what is expected." Just three years ago, 45 percent of legal departments surveyed by the authors were attempting to consolidate their work to a fewer number of firms. Most said it was an effort to lower rates. When done, however, the opposite occurs. The more work a firm does for a corporate legal department the higher their rates.

Why? "Decreasing the number of potential firms from which to source legal work also limits competition," the report says. One way to stem this is that companies combine "consolidation with a panel mechanism." Consolidation may also be viewed as lowering corporate internal operating costs and increasing the possibility of "closer, strategic relationships with law firms."

Finally, no worries if one company pays you more per hour than another for the same work. "On average, 85 percent of lawyers billed at different rates for different companies for similar types of work." This held true across all practice areas.

This report has more than 50 pages of data sorted by firm size, years of practice, practice area and city. I have been able to give you only highlights here. If you have questions specific to your market, firm, or practice area, don't hesitate to contact us. The report segments out the work done for insurance companies versus for their insured's.

Chapter 2:
Key Marketing Performance Indicators

— ◈ —

A client recently asked if we could help them develop a scorecard for marketing. I replied, perhaps too quickly, that we could develop a checklist that might prove helpful, but that after 30 years of owning my own consultancy (and other businesses) the scorecard that matters most comes not from your law firm marketing consultant but from your accountant, your own W-2.

That is not to say that ethics don't matter, that pro bono work is not essential, and that creating a deliberate marketing culture, cross-selling program and diversity aren't requisite, only that they must rest upon profitability.

Accountants Stephen Mabey and Colin Cameron, writing in *Law Practice* said, "Increasingly, management is developing and tracking KPIs for the business development side of firms."

We think their metrics have merit and plan to adopt several. We translated a chart they published into a narrative of metrics you might consider below:

Client Growth Rate

This is a simple measurement to quickly determine if your practice's client base is growing or whether growth in revenue has all come from existing clients. This helps firms to focus their business development spend accordingly.

This is the ratio of the number of clients that the firm handled its first matter in the past 12 months to the total number of active clients (active can be defined as having handled a matter in two of the past three years).

Average Fee per Client

You would track this to see if your client's legal spending with you is growing, flat or declining. It allows you to think about whether the change is rate-driven, client-driven, etc., and then you can respond accordingly.

This is the fee revenue for the year divided by the number of clients billed during the year.

Average Fee per New Client

Firms use this indicator to measure whether the clients being added are contributing to the overall revenue growth as it is, compared to the same ratio for existing clients, from a cost-of-doing-business perspective. In the long term, firms want to generate more revenue from fewer clients.

This is the related fee revenue for the year divided by the number of new clients (clients that the firm handled its first matter for in the past 12 months).

Number of Matters per Client

Firms use this as another indicator of growth because of the focus on existing clients and the ease and lower cost of generating work from them, compared with searching for and landing new clients.

This is the ratio of number of matters billed to the number of clients billed and is calculated by dividing the former by the latter.

Client Retention

Again, firms use this as another indicator of the health of the practice because of the focus on existing clients and the ease and lower cost of generating work from them, compared with searching for and landing new clients.

This is the ratio of number of clients billed in the last 12 months to the same clients that had been billed in the 12 months before that.

Growth in Top Clients

Firms, while growing the business, also want to make sure they don't become over dependent on any one client or small group of clients that could adversely impact the firm's finances if those clients left. Also, firms want to understand where the bulk of their fees are coming from and where they should focus the bulk of their business development efforts.

This is the ratio of fees billed to the top 100 clients (number can be adjusted to size of firm) in the past 12 months to the fees billed to the top 100 clients in the 12 months prior to that.

Dormant Client percentage

Clients that you once had are the easiest ones to pursue for new work, so this is important for that reason and also as an early warning sign of whether you have a quality-of-service issue to follow up on.

This is the ratio of the number of clients that the firm has not handled a matter for in two of the past three years to the number of total clients.

Certainly the numbers will generate discussion in your firm. The key will be to track them over time and use them to evaluate progress against your firm's business and marketing goals.

Chapter 3:
Your Most Valuable Asset:
Your Network

— ◆ —

How to Build, Maintain and Evaluate
Your Business Contact Network

*"In today's complex society of comparably skilled, interdependent people,
it is more true than ever that success is less a function of what you know
than who you know and who knows you."*

Dr. Ronald S. Burt
Chairman, Department of Sociology, Columbia University

The average business professional has a network consisting of many
hundreds of individual contacts. Few professionals recognize the true size and
value of their networks, however. The best at business generation regularly

evaluate and do maintenance on their network to ensure its effectiveness for business development and retention.

In this article, we discuss how business networks function, what makes some relationships stronger than others and how to evaluate and create a robust community of influential contacts so you can efficiently achieve your goals.

A professional social network is a group of individuals who are in contact with one another and who serve each other as an unpaid labor source furthering their mutual business interests.

There are three kinds of contacts in your network:

- Everyone you know
- Everyone you have ever known, and
- Everyone who knows you (but you don't know them)

The first group is where we focus most of our attention. It's the easily-met people, the people to whom you feel closest, including family, colleagues, neighbors, and friends.

The second group is the one most professionals tend to ignore. "Everyone you have every known" are the contacts that you have allowed to fade over time, people you once knew well but no longer see often, if ever, or feel close to. This group – former neighbors, past customers or clients, someone you "did a deal with last year," classmates, a person who served on a committee or board with you – is a group worth focusing on.

Research shows that professionals often get key information, access to scarce and critical resources, some of their best leads and referrals from this second group. That's because these people are most likely to know about opportunities unknown to you. This makes it fair to say that a large measure of the future success in business lies with those from your past.

The third group of contacts is important in another way. They are a resource you have, but of which you are unaware. You become aware of them by that unexpected phone call or email with the familiar beginning: "I was taking with your friend, Mary Jones, and she said you would be just the person we need to handle our new joint venture," or "I don't believe we've met, but several people I trust have said that we would be lucky to have you help with our new venture."

One of the goals in designing your network is to emphasize this third kind of interaction, commonly called the "power-" or "endorsement-referral" so that your network, rather than you directly, does the work of furthering your interests. How do you accomplish power-referrals? Maintaining contact with members of your network and by clearly communicating who you are, will demonstrate to those contacts over time the specific applications of your expertise. ◆

What Do You Get from Your Network?

Three benefits come from your network: referrals, access and information.

Most professionals think of their networks only as a source of new business referrals. And, often they decide against furthering a relationship with a new person they meet because they don't feel they can refer business back to that individual in return for getting a referral.

Given the physical limitation on where you can appear in person, most business opportunities are going to come to you through referrals. However, while referrals are the greatest benefit a network can provide, they are the most difficult to obtain and their frequency and timing nearly impossible to predict. And, they are not the only benefit that you give or receive from your contact network. Our experience with professionals over the decade's shows that of 100 interactions (contacts you make with your network), 99+ percent will involve something other than a referral.

Far more common than new business referrals, networks provide you with access to resources. Members of your network can provide you with access, directly or indirectly, to experts or suppliers you may not have previously known and whom you need to successfully complete a project or write a winning proposal. You can provide the same access in return. Out of 100 interactions with your network our experience is that a handful will involve providing access.

The third benefit of your network is information. Nearly all of the time, it is information that you are providing to members of your network and what you get in return. Study after study shows that consistently providing relevant information is associated with increased success, specifically greater client/customer satisfaction, higher billing and collection rates.

Realistically, there are severe limits on the volume of information you can use, develop independently or manage intelligently while practicing your profession. You can only read so many blogs, books, magazines, newspapers and can only attend a limited number of public events and social functions. But your contacts are reading, hearing and remembering information you'll never otherwise get. They are an army of people processing information, and you can develop your network so you can rely on them to pass to you the information that they find that may have implications for you.

A contact in your network may warn you of an impending problem of which you are unaware, such as financial problems with one of your clients or suppliers, a tentative sales agreement or the imminent resignation of a key individual with the company. Your contact network gets significant information to you before it's generally known, before it becomes public knowledge, and that can give you a competitive advantage. They key is to make sure your contacts know what's important to you.

Who to Network With

Obviously you can't network with everyone. Some people will be easier to network with than others. How do you identify those individuals with whom you are most likely to make contact and subsequently "network"— exchange information, access and referrals?

First, it is essential to realize that only one or two new contacts can be added to your network at any given time. The reason: there are certain essential circumstances and efforts required to solidify a new contact and maintain existing ones in your network.

Frequency

The first step in making a successful new contact is frequency. Any good relationship requires attention. If you meet someone for the first time and decide that you want to attempt to bring them into your network you will need to make contact with them six to eight times over a period of about 60 days to solidify a relationship with this person.

After 60 days, it will require monthly contact for another six months or so, and then I'd recommend at least quarterly contact from then on.

This frequency of contact may seem heavy and unprofessional. However, "contact" is not limited to face-to-face meetings. Contact can take the form of, among other things: personal notes, texts messages or emails; social media contact (LinkedIn and Facebook updates), mailing a relevant newspaper article or forwarding a relevant blog post; a business lunch; a holiday greeting card; seeing someone casually at church, a sporting event or at a club or civic meeting; sending one of your firm's publications or news bulletins.

Shared Attributes

If you can establish frequency of contact, one of the following two situations must also be present in order for the relationship to have a chance of blossoming and then continuing. You must either have what sociologists call "structural equivalence" (defined as having a third party or issue about which you share a strong common feeling such as shared religion, political views or commitment to a social problem) or "attribute homophily" (defined as common attributes with your contact).

The most compelling form of attribute homophily is similar socioeconomic status – similar income, education and occupational prestige. Other common attributes which you might share with a contact which make it easy to network are: age; marital status; offspring; geographical location; race; sex; physical appearance; sports and hobbies, and leisure activity.

If you can maintain frequency of contact with a new member of your network, but lack common attributes, the relationship is likely to prove difficult. In cases in which you have structural equivalence but few attributes in common the chances of a relationship burgeoning is quite slim. ◆

Not all Contacts, No Matter How They Appear on the Surface, Are Worthy

It is important for you to quickly assess a new contact's value to your network. To do this you must evaluate both their "networking ability" and "networking willingness."

There are three attributes to look at in determining a new contact's networking ability. They are diversity, prominence and size. Ask yourself these questions to evaluate networking ability:

- Diversity—does your contact have a varied contact base of its own? You don't want to know a bunch of people who all know everything about each other; you want to know a bunch of people who do not know each other.
- Prominence—do members of your contact's network seek or follow his or her advice?
- Size—how many people are in their network?

A new contact must have a high degree of network willingness or have expressed a desire to develop such willingness for you to try to network with them.

The three characteristics of willingness in networking are a sense of interpersonal debt, power and frequency of sharing. Your new contact may have influence (power) over a diverse and large network. Unless they frequently and enthusiastically share access, information or referrals from that network with you the relationship is out of balance. Further, the contact must realize that if you provide a referral, information or access, that you expect the same in return. This creates the foundation upon which networking is built—trust. ◆

Paying Back an IOU

When your new contact provides you with information, access or a referral you must pay them back. This creates trust.

While you must pay back an IOU you should not pay it back immediately. Express first that you understand your indebtedness and then take time to pay it back properly. This makes your networking relationship dynamic. Also, it's important to understand that if one person becomes to over-indebted to another they often will give up trying to reciprocate. Don't overwhelm people; spread what you have to offer around.

Also remember that a valid networking arrangement may involve receiving a new business referral from your contact and returning important information or access in return. Networking is not a quid-pro-quo. It is a scale that is always slightly out of balance, but each side is attempting to build up value for the other. And, it's perfectly fair to ask for something in return when someone has an IOU outstanding.

In summary, here are the questions to ask when evaluating your current network contacts or when considering adding others to your network:

- Can or am I maintaining frequency of contact?
- Are we or do we think the same?
- Do I know anyone or numerous other people who already know this person?
- Are they able to network?
- Do they want to network?
- Does this person show a sense of interpersonal debt and attempt repayment?

Many of the best networkers make these evaluations informally. Most all can profit by sitting down a couple of times every year to look at where they are spending time, spreading information and providing access. Particularly helpful is identifying those with whom you have recently lost contact and re-contacting them. Almost universally, they are excited to hear from you and have information or an introduction of value to share. A good way to find lost contacts is to look back at your docket or calendar one and two years ago to see who you were interacting with most frequently then.

Chapter 4:
Trade, Community and Charitable Group Participation

——— ◆ ———

Regular Attendance at Trade and Community Group Meetings: That's Just Square One

Just attending the regular meetings of trade groups and community organizations, and a working committee, is not enough. Lawyers need to do more than that to generate the credibility needed for members to hire or refer them.

One of my employment lawyer clients said recently that for two years now he has been religiously attending his Chamber of Commerce's committee on workforce issues. The committee includes employers he can and would like to represent and others he thinks can make referrals on his behalf. He said he has received no work, "even though I mention to everyone at the meetings exactly what I do. It's clear."

Asked if he ever invited anyone on the committee to a separate lunch or coffee, if he had ever had a one-on-one discussion outside of the formal committee meetings about how to mutually support each other's business objectives, he answered "No."

That's the missing link, the step most lawyers fail to take. And, it's essential if you are to get results from community and trade group membership—having individual meetings outside of the group itself to discuss how to support your mutual business interests. All professionals, not just lawyers, need to have these meetings. Discover the other person's business goals and see how you can help him or her. Then explain your business goals and discuss how the person might help you. ◆

What Puppies and Trade Groups Have in Common

When I was president of our local humane society, I was saddened and surprised at how common it was for people to surrender pups about 12 months of age at the shelter. Frustrated owners commonly said they could no longer stand their pet's chewing and other mischief. What we knew and tried to explain to them was that the dogs were just a few months away from naturally settling down into sweet adults.

Clients have asked us how long it will take for a new trade group membership to pay off in new clients or referrals. Like the maturation of a puppy, the answer is about 18-24 months.

Any work or referrals you receive in the first 12 months after you join a group will be by luck. A small matter might develop in the first six months. Don't give up just yet.

Here's why: most all members of the group already had other lawyers (or had other lawyers in mind) when you joined. Certainly, it takes time in meetings, making speeches and participating in other activities within the group for them to get to know you and understand how you might help them. And they will still send the next matter to their existing counsel out of habit before deciding to give you a try. (Don't forget the other meetings outside of the group's meetings I discussed in the preceding article, too.)

Our experience is that most lawyers and firms give up on memberships a bit too soon. Don't join a new group for business development purposes absent a two-year commitment. ◈

Poll Reveals Why Firms Should Invest the Time and Money Required to Create Alerts, Seminars, Attend Trade Shows and Visit Clients

Why should firms spends tens of thousands of dollars and hundreds of attorney hours year-after-year writing alerts, developing trainings and client seminars, discussing their client's business strategy, visiting client offices and touring client facilities, attending the key meetings and shows their clients attend so they are fluent in and understand a client's industry?

Those are staples in the law firm marketing plans we write for local and regional law firms.

"A client relationship is not a one-way street of the client paying and a firm providing legal services. Clients expect you to add to the relationship—bring new insights, help avoid costly risks, leverage lessons learned to improve efficiency, help in ways you haven't helped before. **Your investment is the cost of new business.** Clients want to invest –financially and emotionally– in equally invested firms. If clients sense a lack of investment, the work will be bid out," wrote Michael Rynowecer of BTI Consulting recently.

Firms that invest in their clients, Rynowecer wrote, "are enjoying quantum leaps– 6 percent to 11 percent higher growth– in performance and earning more business than before.

"The challenge for any firm is to stay one step ahead of clients' goals and outpace competitors looking to unseat you as a client's primary provider," Rynowecer said, adding that "Legal advice is widely available. Targeted guidance meshing with clients' specific needs is the rare four-leaf clover clients seek."

The alternative: compete on price. That's fine as long as you are the cheapest in town, but when the time comes that you're not, and that time inevitably does come, your clients have no incentive to stay with you.

What does a firm gain from the time and money these marketing efforts require? Well, your clients invest in your firm's success in return.

According to a poll of in-house lawyers by Rynowecer's BTI Consulting, 41 percent of clients do it in the single most important way any professional can help another professional– by enthusiastically referring you and your firm to a peer. All of us know nothing is more powerful or valuable than a personal recommendation. ◆

Five Tips for Successful Joining

Most young lawyers have been told by a gray-haired mentor to "join something" to jump-start or begin their business development efforts. Many lawyers who follow that advice eventually wonder if they joined the right group or club and how to evaluate the time and effort they have put into the organization. Eventually, even veteran lawyers question the business development value of groups in which they have been active for prolonged periods.

Here are five basic tenets that underlie successful joining. Follow them to make sure you make the most of your own time and your law firm's marketing dollars.

Join a group in which you have a real interest. If you love animals, join the humane society. Don't join the cancer league just because the firm received a letter seeking a lawyer as a board member, unless you have a genuine interest in the disease. If you aren't interested in the industry or community issues addressed by the group, or in the cause supported by the nonprofit, your lack of genuine motivation will quickly become apparent to those you meet. Non-lawyers use anecdotal qualities—timeliness, commitment, enthusiasm, follow-through, etc.—to determine your legal acumen and as evidence of how you would handle their legal matters. If you're not truly motivated about the group you joined, you will make impressions about your client service and legal abilities that are the opposite of what you intended.

Attend group meetings religiously. If you don't, you will not meet people frequently enough to make a lasting impression. If you miss more than three monthly meetings in one year, you might as well have skipped them all. People who get to know you through regular meeting attendance will often wait until a meeting they expect you to attend to pass along information or a referral. Miss the meeting and you miss out.

Get on a working committee and take a leadership position. This lets you establish credibility with prospects and referral sources as you work to further the group's goals. If not a bar group, this also can provide reasons to make contact with people with known legal needs without worrying about your state's in-person solicitation rules. An example is a health care lawyer we represented who headed a trade group membership committee. Her job on the membership committee was to call all newly hired hospital and clinic executives in her state—perfect prospects for her services—on behalf of the trade group to invite them as her personal guest to the next monthly meeting.

Evaluate the members and culture of the overall group and your working committee. Confirm that they joined the group to network and that business development is accepted, if not expected. There are groups that openly discourage marketing. Avoid them. Remember, we're talking about groups you've joined for business development, not purely social purposes.

After a few years, you will feel the point of diminishing returns. When it comes, leave the group and find a new one. Key remaining group members who know you well will represent your business development interests after you're gone. ◆

Best Practices If You Buy a Table at That Charitable or Bar Event

Should your firm buy a table at a charitable or bar function? Should you put an ad in the dinner program? If your firm does this, what can be done to maximize the value of your investment?

Over the years, our law firm marketing effectiveness surveys have shown that nearly 70 percent of firms use tables at charitable and bar events for marketing purposes. About half report they receive cases, directly or by referral, as a result of contacts made or enhanced upon at such events.

Of course, existing and potential clients and referral sources need to attend the event for it to make marketing sense. Obviously, there is no way to determine exactly who is going to be at the event in advance. But a quick review of the members of the governing and advisory boards of the sponsoring organization and of the past event sponsors will give you an idea of who is likely to attend. You should attend if the directors, advisors, and obvious supporters and suppliers to the sponsoring organization—and those they will attract and invite to the event—are the kinds of contacts that will help your firm's business development.

After the event, add the names of people you and other lawyers met to your firm's mailing list to ensure ongoing contact.

It's bad form to buy a table (often with your firm name prominently displayed on a sign above the centerpiece) and have empty seats for everyone there to see. So, only buy a table, or half a table, if you can fill the seats with lawyers from your firm who WANT to be there. Charity dinners are not for everyone, so if only one or two of your lawyers want to attend, scale back the number of seats you buy. If you know other lawyers in other firms who are referral sources (or clients) who like these types of events, you can buy seats and invite them as your guests at your table. Or, if you know a non-competing or other professional services firm might like to split the cost of a table, consider buying an entire table, obtaining the right to a dinner journal ad in the process, and sell off several seats to the other firm. This is not tacky. Many firms do it. For example, I buy seats at a law firm's table every year at a leading bar event. They get the ad rights, with my help, and my wife and I get a seat at a good table in the middle of the room rather than by the back wall, which is where I would have to sit if I bought individual tickets.

An ad in the dinner journal is a nice touch. Try to make it entertaining or memorable. Use professionals to create it. For example, at a recent ACLU dinner we created a simple ad with the headline, "One legal bill is more important than any other we have ever seen." Beneath it appeared the Bill of Rights and underneath that was our client's logo. Our client reported several people came up to them during the event and remarked about the ad. It served as a conversation icebreaker. ◆

Make It Easy for Them to Remember Your Name

I met a university president during a recent business meeting. As I shook his hand, I said my name in introduction and handed him my card. He said "hello" in return—and not a word more.

This was the first time we'd met. I knew his name, first and last, but by failing to introduce himself to me, I had no idea how to address him during the meeting. (Is he Robert, Bob, or Bobby?) Nor did I know how to address a note thanking him for taking the time to meet with us. So, we had to call his office afterward and get all of that information. Business cards weren't part of his meeting repertoire either.

Perhaps a university president can get away with doing this because so many people are seeking the time and favor of a chief executive or pass it off as academic quirkiness. However, a lawyer, accountant or any other professional who depends on word-of-mouth referrals simply cannot.

So always say your name clearly and slowly when meeting people, even those you have met once or twice before. And introduce yourself this way, "Good morning, I'm Bob, (pause) Bob Weiss."

Repeating your first name increases the likelihood those with whom you are developing relationships will hear it and commit it to memory. And after meeting someone for the first time, take the initiative and send him or her a short personal note or quick e-mail if you're expecting the relationship to continue.

Make sure you can offer something of value if you do follow up—an introduction, information or invitation that affects their business or personal lives. ◆

Marketing Requires Patience
Because Results Are Not Immediate

If you, your practice group or your firm is ramping up a formalized marketing effort don't expect to see significant or direct results any time soon.

Be ready to wait anywhere from 12 to 18 months for new business development efforts to start paying off. There are two reasons this is true. I'm not talking about personal injury or consumer-based practices here, but corporate, transactional and defense firm marketing. First, nearly all prospects you will convince to send you future matters already have lawyers or firms serving their needs. Your new clients, before actually engaging you, likely will critically watch their existing lawyer's or firm's performance and billing on current matters before giving you or your firm a try. Second, while new clients may want you to represent them in their next transaction or when their next dispute arises that may not happen for many months.

The exception: an immediate or new need that the client doesn't think current counsel can handle.

The lag between selling your new clients and actually getting substantive work from them is why firms and lawyers must commit both the time and the funding for an ongoing marketing program. That's why you have to be consistent in your advertising and not just buy a few ads that run one month and are never seen again. It's why you commit to a series of ongoing educational seminars, or to an ongoing stream of news alerts, and have an ongoing presence and prominent participation in key community and trade groups.

Otherwise, your new 'clients' will forget your interest in representing them along with the reasons why you should be their lawyer before they have the opportunity to send work to you. ◆

Questions to Ask Before You Pay to Join a New Industry Group

Time is one commodity few lawyers have in excess. As such, careful consideration must be taken when selecting a trade organization to join to help grow your network.

Our clients consistently report anecdotal evidence supporting trade groups as excellent venues for business development. Their remarks are confirmed by our national marketing effectiveness surveys with more than half reporting that they get work directly and by referral from trade groups.

However, some trade groups seem far better than others when it comes to the ease with which lawyers can establish relationships with referral sources and prospects that eventually lead to significant business. As a result, we have recently investigated what characteristics of a trade group appear indicative of fertile ground for business development.

Here are the three most important questions to have answered before you pay membership dues, sponsor an event or become a volunteer. You can find most of this information online at the group's website.

First, can attorneys be active members? If vendors are not allowed to attend regular membership meetings and participate on committees, the organization is far less effective for business development. This is a litmus test; avoid groups in which your lawyers cannot be participating members.

Second, do they have annual, semiannual or monthly meetings? The best groups have monthly membership meetings; quarterly is acceptable if most all members attend religiously. Frequency of contact is the key to establishing meaningful relationships and therefore, the group must meet regularly. Absent regular meetings, results can't happen. Groups that meet only twice annually are problematic, unless they have working committees that meet regularly in the interim.

Third, do they publish a newsletter or magazine, hard copy and/or electronic, which is sent to members? If yes, can lawyers write guest columns on industry issues? Do they accept advertising? You should advertise and write if you can.

Your final step in the analysis of a group is to determine if those who attend and serve on committees can actually buy your services and refer or introduce you to people who can. Avoid groups where the majority of participants do not make decisions. ◆

Charitable Solicitations: Saying "No" Gracefully

How do you graciously decline solicitations for local charities, including those made by clients and referral sources, which unexpectedly contact your firm for monetary support?

A best practice is to have an annual budget designating what your firm will spend and which groups you'll support each year. Budgeting in advance makes it easy to decline unexpected donation requests. You can decline by letter, e-mail or voice mail, whichever is most appropriate in light of your relationship to the group or person making the request. A number of marketing directors and consultants from around the country contributed to the language and messages below. Consider using these points when declining to make a donation:

- Thank you for your letter/request that we participate in this year's "whatever."
- We appreciate the good work your organization does to support "our community's children/hungry citizens/abandoned companion animals." (This part of your message is key—you don't want your response to appear to be boilerplate.)
- We will not be able to "participate/contribute" to this year's "dinner/luncheon/capital drive/golf tournament" because our firm has already allocated its donation dollars for the year.
- We set our budget for donations in the fourth quarter. If you are going to be involved again with "name of group" next year, please let me know in the fall. We wish you the best of luck in your fundraising efforts.

Be prepared for a call back from the organization, client or referral source asking what the firm's donation guidelines are and how the organization can better position a solicitation next year. If you have guidelines, such as "we only give to programs that support education in our community," that can prove helpful. Most firms also require that an attorney (or the client/referral source) be seriously involved with the organization.

Also, you should ask that the firm's donation be recognized in the organization's newsletter, on its website and at the event with a banner through an advertisement in the program and/or by recognition from the master of ceremonies. ◆

Policies to Ensure Charity Tables Contribute to Business Development

One of the most effective tactics that our marketing effectiveness survey shows leads to work directly and by referral is buying sponsorships that include seats at tables at legal, trade group and charity events. Budgeting and ensuring you get the most from each event is critical. The best events are increasingly expensive.

Here's a policy your firm might consider to ensure spending on tables, sponsorships and dinner program ads contribute to business development goals and that your key attorneys fill the seats that are purchased (perhaps along with clients that are targets for cross-marketing of your firm's services).

- Attorney(s) requesting the sponsorship is responsible for filling the table and required to submit a proposed guest list along with the sponsorship request. Requesting attorney(s) must attend the event.
- Attorney(s) is required to state why/how the sponsorship will contribute to the firm, their practice group and their own individual business development objectives.
- If cancellations occur, it is the responsibility of the requesting attorney(s) to find substitute attendees.
- A written follow-up report from the attorney is due within 15 days of the event evaluating the sponsorship, how well it met its objectives, who attended and how the attorney(s) followed up afterward.

NOTE: Your marketing partner, staff or consultant should not be charged with actually filling tables. That's completely up to the requesting attorney(s). It is the marketing folk's job to help attorneys with program book advertising, the sponsoring/host organization's website recognition, public announcements by the host organization and to brainstorm with the attorney about who to invite and what kind of follow-up activities would be appropriate. ◆

Seven Considerations When Asked to Buy an Ad in an Association Directory

Every year our clients are asked to advertise in printed and online association directories that, at first glance, appear to perfectly target to referral sources and clients. For a variety of reasons, we think these ads are of questionable value and do not recommend their purchase. Below we discuss why the ads are not a good investment and suggest alternatives that will allow you to accomplish your goals.

Use of hard-copy directories is significantly declining. Nearly all directories that are published are also available online on an association's website. While there are no studies we can cite regarding hard-copy association directory usage, we know that the most commonly used hard-copy directories, the Yellow Pages, have seen their use drop dramatically—80 percent according to one ABA survey—since the advent of the Internet. The same is true of the hard-copy edition of a directory most practicing lawyers today once regularly leafed through, the venerable Martindale-Hubbell. In fact, studies show that the majority of Internet searches, including those to your own firm's website, are for contact information—e-mail, phone number and physical address. The same is likely true for association directories that members once used extensively. Today, members go to the association website or to online local directories, to get phone numbers, e-mail links and physical addresses, if they are not finding it first directly online. Also, everyone realizes that online directories are more up-to-date than the annually published hard copy.

Even those using the hard copy directory probably won't see your ad. The problem with ads in hard-copy, alphabetically organized directories is that they often appear in sections preceding or following the various alphabetical lists of members. If users are looking up a member with a name beginning with B, how would they ever run across your firm's ad that appears after those members with names begining in S?

Often, associations organize ads or vendor lists into special sections tabbed into the back or front of the directory. This is not logical and helps advertisers little—it transforms a membership directory into a membership-directory-with-a-special-advertising-section of vendors attached.

Exceptions to this thinking concerning a printed association directory you believe has strong usage are:

- Buying an ad on the back cover or better yet, an ad on the front cover if it's allowed. Everyone looks at the directory, either the front or the back, before they open it to confirm they've got the correct publication in their hands. Don't buy an ad on the directory's spine. We have surveyed hundreds of law firms consistently over the years, primarily firms practicing personal injury, which have spent millions of dollars for ads emblazoned on the spines of directories. We don't know exactly why, but ads on the spines of directories just aren't seen.

- Negotiate the purchase of small billboard-like banner ads on the top of, say, every 10th page in the directory. This means users will see a brief message about your firm as they use various alphabetical sections of the directory during the year. This is a great idea, but eventually competitors see the value in it and want to do it too. The coordination of placing ads at specific intervals can become a nightmare for the association. It has led to associations discontinuing the program after a few years. But, it's worth a try if you can be first to suggest it to the association approaching you.

Some firms will say, "Yes, but we want to support the association. We view the directory ad as a contribution so we don't care about the return on investment."

We certainly understand your desire to support an association key to your firm's success, and we hope in which you actively participate since our marketing effectiveness surveys show trade groups are one of the most effective tactics lawyers can employ. BUT, we recommend you buy advertising space in the association's periodical—the monthly newsletter or quarterly magazine. Skip the membership directory.

Many associations, of course, have moved all of their publications on-line in recent years. That sensibly saves them money. It speeds distribution of information and increases relevance. Buying ads on the association's website or e-newsletter is a viable alternative to a print ad.

— ◈ —

Chapter 5:
Client Entertainment

❖

Ensuring Your Firm's Sports and Theater Tickets Are Used Effectively

Recently, one of our clients was sitting with her firm's largest client in her firm's seats at a baseball game. She turned to the young man seated next to her and asked how he got his ticket for that night.

Our client was asking because the young man sitting next to her was in a season-ticket seat owned by her law firm. The young man was "shockingly dressed" and inebriated. He was a stark contrast to the law firm partner's guest. Our client described the situation as "awkward."

Our client learned that the young man's father had been given the tickets the day before by a neighbor. We later determined the neighbor was a client of the firm. The young man and his friend left the game early—well before the seventh inning stretch—announcing loudly and needlessly to those around them that they were going to check out the downtown night-club scene, our client reported.

Our national survey of marketing effectiveness shows that many firms buy season tickets as part of their business development efforts. Routinely, firms debate the effectiveness, efficiency and cost of these tickets. We regularly hear stories of tickets gone begging, or when given away like this being passed along by firm clients to their own customers or friends. We know of instances where an enterprising client sold two of four tickets received from a firm to scalpers. Baseball tickets, due to the frequency of games, are problematic. Arena and stadium suites also prove difficult to manage after the first season.

It's clear that a substantial portion of seats purchased wind up providing questionable value to law firms. As a result, firms should adopt a ticket policy. Here are some elements you may want to include:

- Your firm's policy should be that lawyers must be present at the game or event with the client or prospect for tickets to be reimbursable or charged to the marketing budget. It does lawyers and firms little good to give someone tickets and not accompany the ticket recipient to the game or event. Tickets aren't gifts—they are opportunities to spend time with clients and prospects, to get to know them on a personal level, to learn what they need and how you can improve and expand your business relationship.

- Many firms worry they won't be able manage season tickets they buy if this is the policy. The answer for many firms has been to have lawyers buy tickets personally rather than having the firm own them. Also, to split tickets owned by the firm with another firm. Many firms we represent now split tickets with CPAs, insurance brokerages or banks.

- Your marketing staff, or the managing partner's legal assistant, can track who gets the firm's tickets and who is taken to the game or event. Can't find someone to go? Give the tickets to a hard-working member of your staff—and then move the cost off the marketing expense line and into HR. ◆

Managing Your Firm's Season Tickets

It's early summer and for many firms it's the season for buying and allocating your season tickets – football, basketball, hockey, concert, and theater. Law firms everywhere are sending in their share of the estimated $30 billion that will be spent this year by businesses on tickets and suites to entertain and cement relationships with clients, prospects and referral sources.

According to a recent article in Forbes, TMS, which handles ticket programs for thousands of companies, including giants like Google, Hewlett-Packard and J.P. Morgan Chase, did a survey revealing 43 percent of tickets were unused or given away at the last minute and not used as intended.

Few partners or marketing directors want to see their business development dollars wasted as revealed by the TMS survey. Here are some best practices to ensure your law firm gets the most out of season tickets:

- Rather than buying a suite for an entire season, find out if your local arena, franchise or cultural center sells "per seat" or "per event" shares of suites. In many cities, companies have been formed and offer such packages. Suite seats make a great impression.
- Buy half or a quarter of the season and sell the remainder to another professional services firm.
- Have a schedule and get those who are interested to sign up for specific events or games well in advance. Have each person report with whom they attended the event. You will need to have a marketing or administrative person manage this list and the reports of who attended afterward. Reports should be provided to your marketing committee/partner for review. The looser your supervision and evaluation of attendees the higher the percentage of tickets that go to waste, in our experience.

Problems arise frequently enough with tickets that the Institute of Finance & Management has published a best practice on the topic saying: "If an employer has purchased season tickets to a sporting event or theater, a policy should specify which employees are eligible for tickets, how the tickets are allocated and whether employees can use the tickets for their own personal enjoyment or only for entertaining clients or business associates."

Keep in mind that clients and vendors have their own policies regarding accepting tickets. This may limit how many seats you decide to buy. Here's Ford Motor Company's policy:

> "You may accept up to two entertainment events (such as a golf outing, or a sporting, theatrical, or cultural event) per calendar year, per supplier, provided that the supplier is in attendance and the event does not require extensive travel or an overnight stay."

We all recognize that the practice of law has always been a relationship business and that it will always be a relationship business. Research by the Direct Selling Education Foundation (DSEF) supports this revealing clients "are loyal to businesses they like and trust."

Spending several hours with clients, prospects and referral sources in an enjoyable setting is one of best ways to accomplish both, DSEF says, adding "Make sure most of your conversations are about others. This shows people that not only are you caring, but also gives you an opportunity to highlight your ethics and values."

Remember, the cost impact of games and events that are less popular and to which you may find yourself holding tickets can be lessened if you use them as a charitable donation to gain a corresponding tax write-off. You can also give them as rewards to outstanding employees. If you do the latter, remember to shift the cost of the tickets out of your marketing budget. ◆

Enacting a Policy to Ensure
Membership Dues Provide a Return on Investment

Firms spend thousands of dollars every year on trade and community group memberships. Some of that money is well spent, but in many cases the lawyers don't participate consistently or meaningfully in the groups and the money is largely wasted.

That's a shame since our bi-annual National Marketing Effectiveness Survey indicates that active membership in trade and community groups is one of the most effective ways to build and maintain a business, defense or plaintiff practice.

We often audit marketing budgets and discover that firms have been paying dues and meeting costs year after year absent any evaluation of the return on investment. To ensure your firm is spending its limited marketing dollars efficiently, we recommend the following membership renewal procedure and standards be established. Explain them to all of your firm's lawyers when they are first asked to join a group.

- Community or trade group memberships will be renewed only after a memo from the participating attorney(s) is received explaining how many meetings were attended, if a committee was joined and/or a leadership role taken. It should be noted what new referral or prospective client relationships were established or what existing relationships were being supported. The number and nature of contacts added to the firm's marketing database should be explained as well.
- Your marketing director, partner or marketing committee should review these memos and be given the authority to approve or deny renewals being paid by the firm.
- The person(s) reviewing each request for dues and meeting costs should be wary of requests for groups that meet infrequently. Monthly is best, but quarterly is questionable because strong relationships cannot be maintained absent frequent contact. The group

must be filled with decision makers who can refer or directly hire your lawyers. The group should accept that members are actively networking to support their business goals. There should be working committees, as well. Ideally, the group should have a publication, printed or online, to which articles are contributed.

There will be times when membership in certain groups should be approved as a matter of general community support. Those memberships, however, are memberships in name only. The expense should be shifted to the firm's charitable budget and out of your marketing budget. ◆

A Model Business Development Expense Reimbursement Policy for Your Firm

Lawyers and firm administrators often ask me to help them develop standards for reimbursement of out-of-pocket expenses associated with individual attorney business development. Law firm partner, Brigid Heid, a client of ours in Ohio, and I developed an excellent policy for standard of review which you may want to consider adopting in your firm. It appears below.

"The firm will consider paying for certain activities such as membership dues, conferences, seminars, sponsorships or attendance at events that meet the following criteria:

- If joining an organization, the organization should meet on a regular basis, preferably no less than eight times per year. The attorney must attend all regularly conducted meetings of the organization.
- Within six months of joining an organization, the attorney must become an active member in the organization by taking a leadership role or joining a committee.
- The organization's membership should consist of individuals who are potential clients or referral sources for the attorney or firm.
- The attorney must report on whether the money spent by the firm for the attorney's business development activity has been worthwhile. An associate attorney should report to a mentor during the semiannual and annual associate review process and shareholders should report to the executive committee prior to approval of the annual budget.

Attorneys should consider reporting on the following:

- Whether the names of new contacts from the organization or meeting have been added to the firm's marketing mailing list and the attorney has sent personal notes telling contacts that they will soon receive firm mailings/notices.

- Whether a meeting or conference was informative. If informative, whether the speakers' remarks were circulated to other lawyers, clients or referral sources in an e-mail or memo. "I thought you'd be interested in a summary of the remarks made at last week's meeting of the (group) by (name of speaker...)."
- Whether those who attended the event or who are active members are possible clients or referral sources for the attorney or firm.
- Whether the attorney has had any follow-up with a new contact (for coffee, lunch, etc.) and discussed how helping each other can accomplish mutual business development goals.
- Whether the attorney has introduced a new contact to another lawyer in the firm or to a friend, client or referral source that may be able to help the contact, even if the need is not legal."

Your managing, marketing partner or a committee should review reports like these before memberships in trade and community groups are renewed.

Chapter 6:
Newsletters, Articles and Blogs

— ◆ —

Law Firm Newsletters:
Custom Content Is Best, Avoid a Canned Service

I was asked recently about law firm newsletters and if there are effective preprinted providers or copyright-free article banks for consumer-direct or business/defense firms.

We draft and lawyers finish custom news alerts, electronic and printed, that create Web traffic and referrals for our clients. Sometimes we employ freelancers in support to write on subjects suggested by recent events or our lawyers. The content creates frequency, reach and results in top-of-mind awareness. We can track calls, e-mail inquiries, website visits and cases directly in response.

Canned non-custom content and stock layouts look cheap and, well, canned. They convey (from our research) that a firm employs a cookie-cutter, less personalized approach to handling cases. We don't recommend you use such a service.

Think about the recipients. What affects their day-to-day lives or business practices? That's the information you put in your law firm newsletter, blog posts and alerts. As our client and friend, Dale Perdue in Columbus, Ohio said, your goal is to "alert or alarm." The basic sales tenet at work here is that people are motivated to buy (to retain) when they feel fear or see an opportunity. ◆

You're Moving!
What's the Timing for Announcing Your Office Move?

How far in advance should you notify clients and referral sources that you are relocating your law offices?

In our experience, as soon as people get a new address or phone they update their records and start using it. So we recommend you send the notice of the move to those who are outside your local area on the Wednesday before the Monday you arrive in the new office and to local contacts and vendors on Thursday. If you send the information out before people should use it, say, by several weeks, recipients become confused. We learned this the hard way—a client once showed up at the new offices the week before a firm moved.

Many of our clients send their move announcement via e-mail. Some take pictures of their new lobby and conference facilities, and the exterior of their new building if it is well known and recognizable.

Don't forget to update your website and search engine local listings with this new information as well. Don't forget to notify vendors.

A new location can bolster the good impressions made through the rest of your law firm's marketing plan. A seamless transition to a new location anecdotally confirms how efficiently and effectively you handle legal matters. ◆

Failing to Check Your Local Listings and Your Business Goes to the Dogs

While checking out reviews and confirming local listings on Google for Alyn-Weiss & Associates today, I learned that a dog owns my business and that we are engineers not law firm marketing consultants.

My business, according to coloradoreviews.us, is owned by Rafferty Walker-Weiss, an Airedale long dead and whose ashes are scattered in our backyard. Rafferty was quite bright. However, I was unaware when I adopted him from a divorcing couple 20+ years ago that he had an engineering degree. I assume it was in civil engineering since he dug holes non-stop in my flower beds. According to our listing on www.coloradreviews.us, we have no website and are operating out of offices we vacated in 2005.

I tell you this true story because the recent proliferation of review sites, directories and the search engine's new focus on providing local search results first makes it imperative that your law firm regularly—at least yearly would be our recommendation for a corporate/defense firm and quarterly for a plaintiffs/consumer law firm—look at what comes up on all of the search engines when the firm's name and its lawyers' names are typed into a search bar. You may be as surprised as I was at what you see on or around your firm's Martindale-Hubbell listings and Super Lawyers profiles. Type in "reviews" or "address" and the name of your firm and lawyers in the search bar and you may be aghast.

If your firm has moved in recent years, your new address may not be reflected. Law firms long ago renamed still see the former firm's name. Lawyers long retired, who have moved on or lateralled in to your organization, are listed at wrong addresses and at their prior firm. New clients, opposing counsel, witnesses, vendors, interviewees may wind up going to or using a wrong address or dialing a phone number no longer in service. Smaller screens on mobile devices make the situation worse since fewer results can be seen absent scrolling. Note that B2B firms we represent now see about 10-15 percent of their site traffic through mobile devices; B2C firms experience a multiple of that—and both percentages are projected to increase rapidly.

If you see anything incorrect you can contact the provider. Coloradoreviews.us had a button near the top that made it easy for me to request changes. If you see a poor review on, say, Yelp, you can consider writing a response. Many of these directory sites are simply amalgamating information they get crawling the Web, according to Bill Fukui, an Internet marketing expert and COO of Page 1 Solutions, www.page1solutions.com. Page 1 has developed hundreds of law firm and fee-for-service medical service websites and is a leading SEO provider in both markets. When Bill's teams begin handling search for clients, they look at about 50 sites and directories, such as citysearch, to clean up and make consistent all local search information. One incorrect listing leads to others, he says. "You have to get them all right."

(You may wonder how any directory came up with my dog's name in the first place. Well, I used to subscribe to magazines using the dogs' names. Rafferty was a liberal, subscribing to *The Atlantic* and *Foreign Affairs* using our office address. He allowed his personal information to be shared with third parties. We then watched as his name was passed on to various other publications and public interest groups—the Democrats asked him for money, The Sierra Club sought his input and membership. I think Visa urged he apply for a credit card. My other Airedale, Emma, was a conservative. Emma subscribed to *The New Republic*. She was solicited by Republicans in the next election cycle and contacted by the Heritage Foundation and U.S. Chamber-related interests. When she got a mailer from ATRA she was really excited. She thought it was from Airedale Terrier Rescue Association. Wrong ATRA, Emma. It was from the American Tort Reform Association.) ◆

Simple, Effective Business Development Using Personal Letters

Most lawyers struggle with their individual business development because they don't reach enough people or they do not contact those people they know frequently enough.

Neither issue is hard to fix. Establishing outreach is no more difficult than taking a couple of hours to create a comprehensive mailing list of your clients and referral sources. Your mailing/e-mail list should include experts, other lawyers including opposing counsel, former colleagues, law school alumni, plus the other professionals you know—accountants, insurance agents, doctors, dentists, pastors, friends and family. Really, this is your holiday card list. Go through your calendar and add to this list those with whom you were in contact 12-24 months ago, but with whom you have lost contact. Make sure each letter urges recipients to keep you in mind.

Maintaining frequency is no harder than writing letters or emails every 90 to 120 days talking about your work and the lessons it provides to others, or the work you seek, to those who are on your mailing list. There is no requirement for a formal newsletter (although they have value and a role in law firm marketing) personal letters will do.

The goal of your personal letter or email is to inform, alert and/or entertain the recipient.

Deals, trials or an explanation of recent matters in which you have become involved are suitable topics. Overviews of changes in the law that may affect those on your mailing list are interesting as well.

For example, a group of litigators recently summarized current cases in which they are involved in a letter they sent about 250 contacts. A highly successful tax attorney I know wrote letters about changes in the tax laws and enforcement trends several times a year. His letters regularly created direct inquiries and referrals. Another experienced trial lawyer who started a mediation practice has filled his calendar using highly-creative, entertaining letters to attorneys. This tactic takes the most time, but is the most successful.

Here are some excerpts from his letters.

The author was attorney Dan Patterson of Denver, a well-regarded mediator and a former president of his state trial lawyers association. The letters communicate on several levels at once and are some of the best and most effective personal marketing letters I have ever read:

> "Thirty-five years ago, the United States, North Vietnam, and South Vietnam took more than a month to agree upon the size and shape of the table around which the Vietnam Peace Talks would occur in Paris. North Vietnam favored a circular table where all sides would appear equal. South Vietnam wanted a rectangular table that would demonstrate there were two distinct sides to the talks. After the negotiations led to peace, the principal negotiators, Henry Kissinger and Le Doc Tho, were awarded the 1973 Nobel Peace Prize, although Tho refused the award, maintaining that his country was not at peace.

> "When you mediate with me, you needn't worry about the size or shape of the table, we've already got that covered and it is nonnegotiable. The good news for you is that the recipients for the Nobel Peace Prize this year have not yet been determined. Settling a case or two might lead to a nomination.

> "I'm looking forward to working with you this year in your peacemaking efforts. Who knows, there may even be a prize in it for you."

> "In 1777, dueling practices were codified by a group of Irishmen in the Code Duello, which set out 26 rules for duels, providing such details as the time of day that challenges could be received, as well as how many shots or wounds would be necessary to satisfy one's honor. Parties to a duel typically acted through assistants, who were known as seconds. Seconds had such responsibilities as setting the time and terms of the duel, loading the pistols, and checking the distance between the duelists.

"The seconds were also required, by Rule 21 of the Code Duello, to attempt reconciliation, first without violence, then after a certain number of shots had been fired. The seconds, then, appear to have been some of the first mediators.

"Please understand that, as a mediator, my lineage may go back to the time of dueling, but I do not follow the Code Duello, other than to work with the parties to attempt reconciliation. No shots will be exchanged, no wounds inflicted, and no parties will be killed. Ah, history might have been so different had I been a second for either Aaron Burr or Alexander Hamilton. Fortunately, I am available to you to help you and your clients attempt reconciliation. Call me to help you resolve your disputes—before it's too late."

Great stuff.

Improve your individual business development efforts by sending letters to a great list of contacts at least several times a year. The proven result will be a greater response than you ever imagined. Dan is as busy as he could ever hope to be.

Attractive e-mails, with graphics, can work equally as well. One advantage of using them is the number of emails opened and clicks to your site can be tracked. ◆

Snail Mail May Be Junk Mail but It Delivers

So you want to save on postage and are cutting back or have switched completely to e-mail distribution of marketing materials at your firm.

Bad idea.

You're losing out on files and referrals, according to our clients, our national surveys and a recent independent report.

The report released by the Direct Marketing Association, confirms what our surveys and clients around the country experience after using boring old snail mail to deliver at least some portion of their firm news and legal alerts to clients, friends and referral sources—spikes in website traffic, jumps in e-mails through the website to the firm and an increase in calls to lawyers. And those results are not confined to plaintiff and consumer practices. It's true for corporate, transactional and defense practices too.

Why is your home mailbox filled with what we all pejoratively term "junk mail"? Well, because it works.

Junk mail from a services provider you trust, which adds value to your relationship with them, which helps you conduct your business affairs, simply isn't junk mail.

"With the capabilities of e-mail and Web 2.0, marketers everywhere have simply lost the love for direct mail." said the DMA, adding, "Direct mail still surpasses e-mail in the most important result of all—revenue generation."

Key considerations and tips to maximize response from your mailings are:

- Frequency, frequency, frequency. In marketing, absence does not make the heart grow fonder. For law firms, quarterly snail mail is best in our experience. Fill the gap between mailings with those pithy electronic bulletins. "Prospects scream to UNSUBSCRIBE at a far greater rate than they scream DO NOT MAIL." the DMA said.
- Use third-party services to clean up your databases. Many mailing houses will run your mailing database through what is known as

the CASS Certification System. This is the system that the U.S. Postal Service uses to validate the addresses you have are indeed valid mailing addresses. The CASS process is usually mandatory with mailing houses and the fee is included if you are using them to mail the piece.

The system does not, however, validate the person on your list—only that the address receives mail.

Another good way to double-check the recipient and address are correct is to run your list through the National Change of Address System (NCOA). This will show who has a forward on their address or if the address is no longer valid.

After going through both the CASS and NCOA processes you will still have mailing pieces returned.

- Have each mailer marked "ADDRESS FORWARDING AND RE-TURN SERVICE REQUESTED." Each piece marked with that and sent to a dead address will be forwarded. (Only if you use first class, not bulk rates.) You will get notice of the new address from the post office, for a small fee per piece. We know your lawyers aren't going to review mailing lists more than once annually, if that. They will not be diligent day-to-day about individual address changes either, so this service is a must-do twice a year. The reason: you've got to do it more often than forwarding orders expire.

Forget multi-subject, multipage newsletters. Hardly anyone reads them. The best practice, in our experience, is to send postcards with short one- or two-sentence summaries of articles or news and give the recipient links to your website for the full story. When planning your mailing, keep in mind that 4.25" x 6" is the largest size that still falls within postcard postage rates and all other sizes will be charged at higher postal rates.

———— ◆ ————

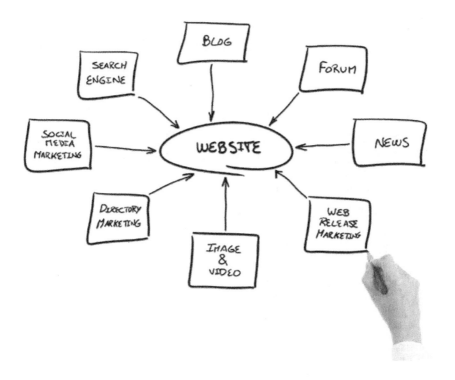

Chapter 7:
Social Media and Websites

— ◆ —

The ABA's Stance on Website Ethics,
Blogging, Ratings and Paid Search

An online marketing strategy should be included in every law firm marketing plan and we advise all of our clients closely follow their state ethics schemes when developing and maintaining websites and blogs. However, only a few states have substantively addressed the Internet marketing era in their rules. The guidance out there is increasing but remains scanty with few states having anything more than a few opinions or amended rules directly addressing the most modern marketing tools. Instead, firms have to look at rules developed prior to the advent of e-mail and online search and apply them as best possible to their sites, blogs and social media, such as a LinkedIn.

The ABA has issued some guidance, including a formal website ethics opinion, Opinion 10-457, http://www.abanet.org/cpr/pdfs/10-457.pdf.

The ABA also appointed a commission to consider rules governing:

- Pay-per-click advertising
- Pay-per-lead arrangements
- Online social networking profiles and e-mail (Facebook, AVVO, LinkedIn, and Twitter)
- Blogs
- Contact Us/FAQ/Ask-A-Question features on websites
- Discussion forums and chat rooms; live chat and website features
- JD Supra document uploads
- Use of case histories

That commission was also "separately considering issues related to rankings and ratings of both lawyers and law firms, as well as the emergence of third-party services that provide information about lawyers and solicits their participation in supplying that information."

In late 2011, however, saying they could not find anyone had been harmed by ratings, citing the costs of an exhaustive study and the likelihood of First Amendment issues, the Commission recommended a "hands off" approach to all of this. As of early 2016, nothing more had transpired. ◆

Studies Confirm Value of E-News and Blogs

A recent study reveals, despite the deconstruction of traditional news media, that people are spending on average nearly 30 percent more time every day accessing news than they were 10 years ago.

Make your firm's communications newsworthy, not self-laudatory, to clients, prospects and referral sources and your law firm marketing plan will have tapped into what The Pew Center for the People and Press study (http://people-press.org/report/652/) has revealed. Pew's biennial study of news consumption says people still spend 57 minutes daily getting news from print and broadcast outlets, the same as they did in 2000, albeit more of that time is spent with TV than print media today. However, Pew reports, people spend an additional 13 minutes accessing news online, 70 minutes in total. That's the most time spent daily since Pew began measuring news consumption nearly 20 years ago.

"This underscores the importance of new ways people find news increasingly from one another," wrote L. Gordon Crovitz in a column in the Wall Street Journal.

Yet another study by American Lawyer Media says 53 percent of in-house counsel expects to obtain more of their industry news and information through new media in the future.

These studies underscore what we advise our clients to do, which is to consistently create online content that is informative, searchable and forwardable. It's a mainstay for every law firm.

The constant, Crovitz said, is "that people want to know what's going on and will find the most convenient, useful and engaging ways to stay informed." ◆

The Modern Overall Firm Communications Strategy

A new survey of law firms of 10-49 lawyers (the size firm and branch offices we commonly work with) reveals 26 percent of law firms are now blogging, nearly double the number that were two years ago, and that 39 percent of those firms have received work directly from their blogs.

The 2015 American Bar Association Technology Survey also reveals 19 percent of firms have received work through LinkedIn and that 90+ percent of lawyers in those firms have a profile on the service.

This article discusses how these social media components fit into an integrated overall firm communications strategy. It also suggests how firms can get even more work from the content created for their blogs.

We urge firms to post:

- Case results and transactions—assuming clients approve
- Firm-centric news—rankings, ratings, awards
- Discussion of recent trial results and appellate decisions—not your own cases but those affecting day-to-day business decisions of your clients and prospects
- Thoughts on lawyering—discussing advocacy and clearly conveying your firm's personality. This is to make you approachable, demonstrate competence and accomplishment, and, most importantly, reveal how you think. How you think is what you sell.

A good example of a law firm's blog is Seattle-based litigation boutique Savitt Bruce & Willey, www.sbwllp.com. (If the whole idea of blogging feels uncomfortable, note that you can create a News/Articles page on your website that—if properly optimized—will function much like a blog.)

Blog posts have an intrinsic promotional weakness that must be addressed. They are passive communications, sitting on the Web waiting to be found. Our recommendation is to find ways to repurpose each and "push" them out to clients, prospects and referral sources.

Specifically, we recommend:

Every time a blog post is written or an article is put up on your website, the firm should create a version of it as a LinkedIn "update." All interested lawyers (or someone with access to all of the LinkedIn accounts of all of your interested lawyers) would then enter the copy into the Update box on their accounts. That means the post will go to all of that lawyer's Connections, to be seen in the Newsfeed the next time the Connection opens his or her LinkedIn account. You can use up to 700 characters to write an Update. Under the Update will appear a link back to the full blog post on your site.

Recently, LinkedIn® added an article feature to its platform. If you author a post/article, just click on "Publish to Post" on the Home page of your profile. Insert a headline and the text and hit "Publish" – all of your Connections will then get your piece via email. Lawyers using this report 20 percent open rates and many "likes."

By the way, we recommend you have an email subscription request box on your blog. In the alterative, an RSS feed will suffice. The problem with RSS sign-ups is they are anonymous. You can't see who is subscribing. Some research indicates RSS feeds are less frequently read by recipients than emails. We urge email over RSS for this reason.

Next, every quarter we recommend the firm pick three or four posts from the blog. One might be firm-centric, one about a case/decision and one about lawyering. Put them together as a newsletter sent to your firm's clients, referral sources and prospects. We fully recognize firms may be reluctant to add to the deluge of email people receive, but you will be able to see how much people like this idea if you execute this strategy properly.

This newsletter could be either an email or a hard copy postcard. Recent research suggests hard copy has a role in the mix of ways you stay in touch with people. That said, most of our clients prefer to avoid the cost of postage and printing and opt for email newsletters.

If sent via email, the newsletters must be CANSPAM compliant and have an unsubscribe feature. Using one of the numerous commercial programs available, such as Constant Contact®, you will get a detailed report after each is transmitted showing the number opened, click-throughs to the firm website, the unsubscribes and forwards. If your firm doesn't have a healthy open rate after trying it a few times, something we have yet to see happen, we'd say drop the tactic. No client of ours has ever stopped doing an e-newsletter once starting it. We find 20 percent of recipients open and read e-newsletters. The legal industry average is 18 percent. One of our clients has a 40 percent open rate. And yes, clients do unsubscribe.

Certainly some people will get your stuff more than once depending on which alternatives suggested above are adopted by your firm. In our experience, ramping up frequency like what we describe above comes without risk. Instead, all firms that have done what we recommend report positive feedback, referrals and retentions as a direct result over time. Client surveys we have done also reveal your clients, referral sources and prospects appreciate being sent information reflecting their interests and justifying why they hire you (because you're AV-rated or a Super Lawyer, or active in a key community group).

We think it all goes back to Dale Carnegie's maxim: "Tell the audience what you are going to say, say it; then tell them what you've said." Frequency and repetition of a message is just basic to strong human relations. It's why you have to tell your spouse and kids you love them, and tell them every day. (As an experiment, try cutting back on frequency of that message and see the reaction!)

The research suggesting direct mail may be better than email for a newsletter comes from a study by three university researchers published in the Journal of Marketing. (Alyn-Weiss employs direct mail as described.) The study analyzed the purchasing habits of customers for auto dealerships via customer surveys and dealership records. It measured the impact of direct mail, telephone calls and email marketing on the purchases and spending of those customers. Additionally, it determined what the ideal frequency was when using the three marketing channels together.

The results of the study indicated that businesses should communicate mostly through direct mail and less via telephone and email. The ideal mixture, according to the research, appears to be 9-10 postal mailings, three phone calls, and three to four emails all over a period of three months. This provided the highest positive impact on the spending of the research subjects, thus indicating ideal points for frequency and advertising mix.

According to co-author Andrea Godfrey, a University of California at Riverside assistant professor of marketing, "... the results are applicable to all types of business, particularly service businesses."

We understand retention and referral patterns and target audiences for most law firms are not the same as for purchases from an auto dealership. We have found consistently over the past 25 years that marketing models that apply to products—for branding, pricing, life cycles, marginal return, etc.—can be directly applied to professional services with slight modifications. In this case, that's why we reduce the frequency a bit, use email a bit more and eliminate phone calls from the mix recommended above.

Interestingly, one of the theories put forth by the researchers in the article is that customers view physical mail as less intrusive than calls or email and thus, are more likely to sit and consider the messages. These results offer strong support for including occasional direct mail in your overall communications strategy.

> *"You can make more friends in two months by becoming*
> *interested in other people than you can in two years*
> *by trying to get other people interested in you."*
>
> **Dale Carnegie**

RICO Lawsuit Against SEO Company

Search Engine Optimization, done right, can support referrals and drive work directly to a law firm and its lawyers. Our national surveys of consumer law firms, litigation boutiques and business law firms reveal this to be true and it's a best practice we include in every law firm marketing plan we write.

Done wrong, as alleged in the RICO lawsuit this link takes you to

http://lawyerist.com/lawyerist/wp-content/uploads/2013/07/FairleyComplaint.pdf,

SEO can cause the search engines to make you invisible to search. This is commonly caused by using so-called "black hat" practices which you can read about by doing a simple search.

SEO is a specialty area of marketing practice. It's hard work that requires ongoing attention. How to best achieve the results you want requires you hire and continually work with an SEO experts who, like any professional advisors, must stay atop of the latest techniques and restrictions. Those experts need to work with marketing consultants like us or, with your resident marketer or marketing partner to ensure whatever content is generated is original and then its value extended as compelling information properly pushed out to clients, prospects, friends and referral sources.

Beware promises of quick results and little work or little monitoring being needed by you or your lawyers to achieve success. Otherwise you'll end up in trouble like the plaintiff in the lawsuit above, or with inane copy like this we saw posted by a well-known national third-party blogging service to a personal injury firm website: "Every day, numerous motorists drive on the roadways. Among them are truck drivers who regularly pass through those roadways to reach their appointed destinations." Can you imagine paying to have someone write that for you? What would a prospective client or another lawyer think of your or your firm when they read it? ◆

Lack of Social Media Presence Is Professionally Perilous

Buyers of professional services self-diagnose their problems and are far into the selection process—60 percent of the way to retention—according to new research further substantiating that a robust online and social media presence is requisite for attorneys.

In addition, being a social media "hold out" is perilous for a professional. It makes you invisible to large swaths of your market and creates the appearance you handle a client's vendor agreements related to cyber-security, e-discovery and issues associated with predictive coding.

Data supporting this comes not from newly-formed hip digital marketing agencies but recognized business community stalwarts, The Corporate Executive Board and Harvard Business. You may want to read the articles and review the data yourself at:

http://blogs.hbr.org/cs/2013/07/the_perils_of_being_a_social_media
_holdout.html?utm_source=feedburner&utm_medium=feed&utm
_campaign=Feed percent3A+harvardbusiness+ percent28HBR.org percent29

http://www.executiveboard.com/exbd-resources/content/digital-evolution
/pdf/Digital-Evolution-in-B2B-Marketing.pdf

◈

Social Media Etiquette:
Tips for Making Sure Your Efforts Are Well Received

Social media has created a phenomenal opportunity for people to share and receive information about their business and expertise instantaneously. While social media has revolutionized the way all professional services are marketed, it has not changed the fact that we must mind our manners. Here are a few tips for ensuring your online efforts are well received.

- Know your technology. Regardless of the platform—LinkedIn®, Facebook®, Twitter®—know what your profile and status updates look like to the rest of the world. Your profile is an extension of your image, both personal and professional. Know what your online presence looks like... everyone else does.

- Regardless of your privacy settings, treat your pages and status updates as public information. Don't post anything you wouldn't want your current or future clients and referral sources to see.

- Regardless of how valuable your message is, the focus will always be on your mistakes. Make sure you proofread your posts. ◆

Clients Expect a Detailed Bio
and Use Online Search to Verify Referrals

Lawyers must invest time in writing detailed biographies on their firm's website. "It really irritates me when a lawyer's online bio or profile is cursory or lacking in detail and doesn't indicate industry experience and include descriptions of and links to key cases," one general counsel told me.

When asked, everyone on a panel at a meeting of general counsel I recently moderated agreed that online searches and "a robust online presence" equal legal guides and online directories when it comes time to look for outside counsel in a particular area or to validate a referral.

Again, write, review and update your bio regularly. Make sure to add detailed new case/trial and/or transaction experiences that will appeal to your clients and which prospects will take into consideration when making a decision to hire you and your firm. And include a short video of yourself—a survey of in-house by HubbardOne showed that lawyers were more likely to be hired if video was present to illustrate demeanor.

In the end, your website bio is a lawyer's most important marketing document. ◆

LinkedIn Nets Lawyer a Six-Figure Fee

We get a lot of questions about whether or not it's worthwhile to participate in social networks such as LinkedIn®. Our advice is always, "Yes, do it and do it now."

Here's proof that it works. We were in Los Angeles speaking about marketing effectiveness and best practices in an annual meeting of an international law firm network. We met a corporate lawyer who got a $70 million international transaction from LinkedIn®. He expects to bill six figures in fees.

Here's how it worked:

The international client did an online search for a Los Angeles corporate lawyer with experience with mergers and acquisitions for companies that have operations in Asia and who spoke Japanese.

The lawyer's LinkedIn® profile showed up in the search results and said he wrote and spoke Japanese fluently.

The client reviewed the lawyer's profile and found out everything he needed to know about the lawyer to hire him.

The lawyer runs three LinkedIn® groups and participates in other industry-related groups. He also has his blog linked to his LinkedIn® account, updates his status and asks for and makes recommendations consistently. This raised his rankings on Google for the search terms the client used.

So is it worthwhile to participate in social networks such as LinkedIn®? Yes, do it and do it now. ◆

Basic Guide: LinkedIn for Lawyers

(The following is a synopsis of a presentation by Phil Nugent, a marketing and business strategy consultant who works with a diverse mix of businesses in the technology, financial and manufacturing industries on effective use of LinkedIn by lawyers. That presentation was to the Rocky Mountain Chapter of the Legal Marketing Association. We have made some changes to the summary written largely by freelance writer and blogger Janet Ellen Raasch, jeraasch@msn.com, a good friend who for many years was an in-house marketing director. It appears here with her permission. Nugent is a non-practicing lawyer.)

The ABA reported recently that 95 percent of its members indicate that they have posted their profiles on LinkedIn®. As you may have read elsewhere in this book, one ABA survey reveals 75 percent of corporate counsel use LinkedIn regularly as a tool to find and vet outside counsel.

LinkedIn is now one of the world's most popular websites. If you would like to be found by potential clients, your LinkedIn® profile has become even more important than your website biography. If you are looking for networking opportunities, your LinkedIn presence and activity have become just as important as your face-to-face networking.

"From the very start, LinkedIn differentiated itself as a site for business, business development and recruitment rather than a social site." said Nugent. "In just 10 years, LinkedIn has gained 225 million users around the world, including 80 million users in the United States.

"More than 173,000 people join LinkedIn each day. It is a great place for many attorneys because the demographics of LinkedIn skew older, wealthier and more-educated than any of the other top social media sites.

"Successful use of LinkedIn as a business development tool has three steps," said Nugent. "First, you must post a complete and compelling profile. All too many lawyers and law firms leave it at that however, and then wonder why LinkedIn is not working as well as they had hoped.

"To achieve success on LinkedIn, you must build a strong network of connections in terms of both quality and quantity," said Nugent. "With this accomplished, you can leverage LinkedIn as a business development tool to find others, to get found and to conduct market research."

Getting Started on LinkedIn

The creation and posting of a good profile is step one of a solid LinkedIn presence. However, it should not be the same as a lawyer's website bio. Instead, it should be designed to satisfy the unique needs of LinkedIn's search algorithm.

"LinkedIn's algorithm uses a metric to quantify profile strength, which has a huge effect on search results," said Nugent. "Different areas of your LinkedIn profile carry different weights. You should aim for a profile-strength of 'all-star,' or as close to 100 percent as possible."

Nugent discussed and gave specific recommendations regarding the algorithm's weights.

Name and title (25 percent)—Do not make the mistake of simply listing a generic job title in this very important space. It should include carefully selected keywords—the keywords that those searching for someone like you are likely to use. The title category can be as long as 120 characters, or about 18 words.

Photo (5 percent)—A profile that includes a photo is seven times more likely to be viewed than one without a photo. Be sure that the photo is both professional and recent.

Summary (10 percent)—Use your summary to tell a compelling story about how you help clients solve their legal problems. This section should include plenty of keywords. It can include up to 2,000 characters, or about 350 words. Spell check is always recommended.

Education (15 percent)

Previous two jobs (30 percent)

Three recommendations (15 percent)

Another smart tactic for promotion of your LinkedIn presence is to customize your profile's URL. LinkedIn automatically generates a random URL, but this easily can be changed to a much shorter version featuring your name. Additionally, you should be sure to add links to your website and blog.

On the "Edit Profile" page you can add content modules that include projects, publications, honors and awards, patents, certifications and languages.

"Throughout your LinkedIn profile, remember that content is king," said Nugent. "The copy should be compelling and should include plain-English keywords that are the same words that will be used by your target market or your ideal clients. These keywords should indicate who you are and what you do. Avoid 'legalese'—unless your clients use it, too."

Once you have prepared and posted a strong LinkedIn profile, you want to make sure that people can actually gain access to it. Go to the "Privacy & Settings" section of your profile and choose the settings that allow "everyone" to view your profile photo and visibility.

Creating a LinkedIn Network

To support a strong LinkedIn profile, you need a strong network. When it comes to building a network, you can pitch as well as catch. This means that you shouldn't rely only upon the invitations that you receive; you should proactively send invitations to those with whom you would like to be connected.

A LinkedIn network works like a big circle, with you in the middle. First-degree connections are direct connections. These are the people you have accepted and who have accepted you. Second-degree connections are friends of these friends. Third-degree connections are friends of second-degree connections. Your level of visibility into third-degree connections is limited, and a request to connect must be routed through the second-degree connection that controls the relationship.

"The quality of your network is important," said Nugent. "If you accept too many random invitations, your network, although large, may not be sufficiently useful. If you accept (and send) too few invitations, you won't be able to use the database as it was designed.

"Before accepting any invitation," said Nugent, "ask yourself if this person is potentially a client or a source for the kind of work you really want to do. Strive for balance between the quantity and the quality of the invitations you accept."

When vetting an invitation, check out the inviter's profile. Is the invitation from a real and (apparently) respectable individual? Does the inviter have quality contacts that might prove valuable? Does the inviter have a large number of contacts? Did the inviter include a personal note with the invitation? "Rely on these factors to determine if it makes good sense to connect," said Nugent.

When sending out your own invitations, start with your existing contact list. Include your firm's partners, associates and staff, members of professional, business and industry groups that you belong to, and referral sources, clients and friends.

"Never allow your network to stagnate," said Nugent. "It should grow continuously. When you meet a new contact, follow up within 48 hours with an invitation to connect on LinkedIn instead of (or in addition to) an email or a written note. To facilitate this tactic among those you meet, consider including your LinkedIn address on your business card."

Using LinkedIn for Research

"A well-crafted LinkedIn network is like a finely tuned sports car," said Nugent. "It's really a waste if you just let it sit in the garage. You should take it out for a spin as often as possible. The more you 'drive' LinkedIn, the more you'll discover its usefulness—and the more you'll realize what a powerful tool it can be on a daily basis."

Your LinkedIn network is essential when conducting pre-interaction due diligence. "You can search your network in order to find out useful information about prospects, their companies, clients, competitors, consultants, referral partners, media sources and employees," said Nugent. "The quality of your results will be determined by the quality of your contacts and the size of your network.

"LinkedIn can help provide answers to many important questions." said Nugent. "These include who is the right person to talk to in a particular organization? What can I discover about this person prior to our meeting? Who else is on their team? Who might be able to provide me with background or an introduction?"

LinkedIn's "advanced search" capability allows you to refine a search by relationship, location, current company, industry, past company, school and language. Search can be further narrowed by groups, years of experience, function, seniority level, interests, company size, Fortune ranking and date joined.

Lawyers who want expanded search capabilities and additional functionality can try a premium membership on a monthly basis rather than sticking with the basic free membership. However, the free membership provides plenty of power for most LinkedIn users.

"LinkedIn has gone from being a novelty embraced by techies to a must-have marketing tool for all professionals who hope to compete in today's marketplace." said Nugent. "By creating a strong profile and a robust network, and by being an active user, any lawyer can vastly enhance his or her online visibility and reputation." ◆

Maximizing LinkedIn's Newest Features

LinkedIn's newest feature—in a just a couple of clicks—let's you easily discover details about who your Connections know and find those to whom you may want to ask for an introduction.

Here's an overview of how it works from the Winston-Salem Journal:

"Until recently, sifting through someone's first-level connections was an unwieldy task, particularly when it's not unusual for people to have in excess of 500 connections. Who has the time to click on all those profiles to see where people work?

Here's what's new and why it's extremely helpful. Go to your first-level connection's profile page. Scroll down to their "Connections" section. To the right of that black box is a magnifying glass, symbolizing your ability to search. Click it.

In the small box that opens up, type in any key word. For example, type "banking." Hit "enter." You will now see their connections with "banking" somewhere in their profile.

Now, look just below the "Connections" black box. It'll show you how many connections met that "banking" criteria AND you'll see a link for "advanced search."

Click "advanced search" and you'll now be able to sort through all of your friend's connections based on a wide variety of criteria.

Interested in connections working for a particular company? Those with a certain job titles such as recruiter, manager, director, vice president or president? It's all searchable now.

The same search criteria are now available for people in your groups."

Been busy and need to catch up on your personal business development? This LinkedIn feature can help you get momentum quickly. ◆

Embracing LinkedIn: Connections

In every law firm marketing plan we write, we recommend lawyers embrace LinkedIn®. We also offer training in how to best use the platform.

As we train, many lawyers ask us: "I have worked hard to create and nurture my contacts, why would I put them out on the Internet for anyone, including other lawyers, to see and potentially use?"

As a general rule, we say you should keep your Connections on LinkedIn open to be viewed by your existing Connections and be thoughtful about who you subsequently add to the list. It makes sense to add and accept competing lawyers who might refer a conflict, who might want to be or have been co-counsel and to whom you'd refer a matter. Lawyers you do not fully trust, who might actively market a referred client, should be avoided. If you're connecting to add value and actively nurture relationships—the true purpose of LinkedIn—you'll get the benefits of helping those you trust and respect without having to worry about who has access to your list of Connections.

To be more specific, hiding your Connections on LinkedIn minimizes the opportunities available to you on the platform and list protection can also be achieved by being strategic about with whom you connect. Here are a couple of reasons why hiding your Connections may not be the best approach on LinkedIn.

- One Goal of Social Media is to Create and Maintain Mutually Beneficial Relationships

The key to being successful on social networks is to "create more value than you capture." one expert said in a recent article we read. On LinkedIn, part of being a giving participant involves connecting like-minded individuals through introductions. For this to be possible your Connection list must be visible to those in your network.

In addition, hiding your Connections can be viewed as "unfriendly." Some people will see that you are not willing to fully open up, participate and help others. So they will not be as helpful when you reach out to them.

This is the same strategy we have taught for years in our networking skills workshops—open your network fully and willingly to those whom you trust and you should expect the same in return. Social media is no different than traditional one-on-one personal networking in this regard.

- Only Your Connections Can View Your Contact List – Not Everyone on LinkedIn

Another aspect to keep in mind is that only those people you've connected with can see your contacts. Since not everyone on LinkedIn has the same access levels to your profile information, you have some control over who can view your contact list without hiding it.

By only connecting with people with whom you have established relationships, you'll have less reason to worry about poaching. If someone you do not trust, like a competitor, wants to connect, simply choose to deny the request and your list will still be protected. In addition, you can also disconnect with people should you decide you are no longer comfortable with them having access to your Connections. When you do this, the person you drop as a Connection is not notified. ◆

Quick LinkedIn® Updates Can Tell a Big Story

Here are some examples of effective Updates on LinkedIn by lawyers from around the country:

"...preparing to defend an employer against an unfair labor practice charge before the National Labor Relations Board."

"...working on a SLAPP motion filed in a prescriptive easement lawsuit."

"...responding to wage & hour audits from the U.S. Department of Labor. The threat of employer audits has come to fruition..."

And, "just completed a private placement for an alternative energy company."

They're effective because they are discrete and discreet. (Ha! Have you ever used those two words in a single sentence?) They show the power of the Updates you can post on LinkedIn. Now, that's new media. ◆

We Paid to Rank High on Google. How Do I Know It's Working?

Our National Marketing Survey reveals that most commercial firms found ranking on Page 1 of Google and other search engines creates new work, directly and by referral. But how do you measure the success of that effort, what is commonly known as Search Engine Marketing or SEO?

Like all marketing ROI (Return on Investment) analysis, monitoring your return from SEO will be imprecise. The reason: clients and referral sources may do a search and wind up on your site, an SEO success, but then send e-mails, forward links to third parties or call you on the phone. None of that will be traced back to their original search. And even if you ask how you were found, we all know the problems of witness recall.

Witness recall aside, you still should measure your SEO efforts as best you can. Here are some basic indicators to consider reviewing.

For each area of practice, use a program to determine where your firm ranks on Google, Bing (formerly MSN), and Yahoo for the phrases for your key types of work. Those three search engines comprise about 90 percent of all searches on the Internet. There are numerous tools you can find online to do this. One is called Rank Checker (www.rankchecker.net), which can be downloaded and used for free through your Internet browser.

To evaluate your websites general performance, make sure you have an analytics program in place. Google Analytics is the industry standard and it's free.

Most analytics programs will give you more information about your site than you can digest. For the trends that develop over time, try to keep your focus on these few things:

- The number of unique visitors to your site. Getting a large and growing number of people to visit your site is indicative but not necessarily the goal. You want the right people to come to your site and take the right action, that being to contact you about doing challenging legal work at your prevailing rate. One thousand visits to your site by people who never engage you is uneconomic. A few dozen visitors, several of whom engage you is economic. You want "buyers" not "shoppers."

- From what sites visitors come to yours. Among other things, how often do you get site visits from the Martindale-Hubbell sites (martindale.com or lawyers.com), often the single largest (and most controversial) expense in your budget? This report will tell you.

- Average time spent viewing. A few minutes is ideal. Visitors enter, they like what they see and they are prompted to make contact—that's what you want, not lookey-loos.

- Bounce rate. A bounce means the visitor went to one page and left your site. That's not good if they're researching your firm, but it is if they already knew your name and were just looking for your phone or email address. Your bounce rate should be about 40 percent. ◆

Some Firms Are Surprised to Learn They Do Not Own Their Websites

Many law firms upgrading their websites are surprised to learn they do not own their online assets. They licensed them to save money upfront years ago.

They are forced to pay their original designer and hosting company substantial additional (often non-negotiable) fees when they want to make a change in who hosts, designs and optimizes a new website. The expensive alternative for many has been to start over from scratch with only some their content salvageable from their original licensed site.

Law firms are not alone in discovering this. Friends of ours in construction, accounting and other professional services firms have run into this problem. In each case, the firms had decided to use new designers to replace sites functioning passively as online brochures. The new sites generate leads and compete for viewership on the Internet.

In short, you want to make sure your firm owns all of its digital assets. Avoid a site on a provider's custom system. This helps you manage costs long term and gives you maximum control of your law firm marketing. You want to have a site with programming code that is "open source," not custom. You want to choose one supported by a large, active and public development community. This allows you to hire anyone you want to work on the site—not just your original designer and programmer. Examples of open source are WordPress and Drupal.

The shift away from traditional media and advertising is inexorable (and is confirmed by our National Marketing Effectiveness Survey of law firms). As firms make ever-larger investments of time and money in their digital assets, the proper handling of these transactions is increasingly critical. ◆

How to Get a New Website Quickly and Within Budget

We recently completed a fully optimized entirely new website for a client in just 90 days, a record time for our team. This is particularly gratifying because we have clients and know of firms that have struggled for up to two years on their sites, and when done have been dissatisfied with both the process and the results.

Here are some reasons why this project went quickly and smoothly.

First, the firm entrusted a small working group of four people to make the design, copy and site navigation decisions. This group confirmed with its executive committee the objectives for the site before development began. Those outside the working group could ask all the questions they wanted, but were not allowed to interrupt/stop the process (participate in working group meetings). This eliminated the many mid-project discussions we've seen where lawyers not fully engaged or on the periphery ask, "Why don't we try this?" or "Why are we doing that?" Reassessment of the strategy and revisiting design decisions repeatedly will dramatically delay the process and often make the final product disjointed.

When new copy was written, a memo was created for the editors. It explained that writing for the Web is not legal writing, and that website copy is organized and must read differently to be effective. This must be clearly understood. A few people outside the working group were asked to edit because of their expertise in a particular area. (Call me if you'd like to discuss what is in this memo.)

The working groups and development team created a clear written time schedule for each phase of the project. The working group and our team had regular, at least twice monthly, conference calls and online meetings to review progress. We agreed and largely held to making the big decisions—home page layout, navigation, images, copy—in no more than one week. The ethics officer was kept informed and turned his reviews around quickly.

Finally, engaged third-party designers and SEO experts we knew were well organized and had experience with legal services.

Yes, there were spirited discussions and tight moments as there always are on such complicated projects. But we got it done on time and on budget. As with any major construction project, we have a punch list, but it's shrinking.

In just a few weeks, we have seen a solid drop in the site's bounce rate. That's an initial indicator that we have a far more functional Web presence. ◆

Having a Comprehensive, Measurable Plan Increases Likelihood of Marketing Success

The chief marketing officer of the country's largest lawyer television advertising agency recently sent a newsletter, one of a series, confirming what we have been telling personal injury lawyers seeking higher case values for years—success lies in having a comprehensive measurable law firm marketing plan addressing online reputation management, personal selling, community relations, database driven communications and your advertising to compete for decent value cases.

Harlan Schillinger, who has been with Network Affiliates since the early 1980's and is a pioneer of effective personal injury lawyer marketing, recently said: "Here's a news flash: the old days of just placing ads on TV and waiting for the cases to roll in are dead.

"The future of the web is on social media. Eventually, these (platforms) may end up replacing your current websites. The other problem with this expectation is that many law firms are expecting the web to create the sort of business their TV campaigns did in the 1980's." "That's not going to happen." Harlan said. I agree. In today's fractured media environment only a multi-faceted approach will work.

Harlan goes onto recommend something else we have long said—that being every law firm must have analytics on their website to have any idea if it's working.

"It's impossible to make intelligent decisions online without having the numbers to back up your decisions. Knowing how your website performs and establishing realistic goals and expectations is the first step to growth." Harlan said.

As we know so well when we first begin working with most referral-based personal injury practices for which we write law firm marketing plans: "Most law firms are completely in the dark in terms of how many visitors come to their website on a monthly basis, how they rank in search engines for key search terms and how many leads their website has actually generated," Harlan said, adding that "Without knowing this information, how can your law firm make an informed decision on how to improve their presence online? Furthermore, without a baseline, how can your law firm set reasonable goals for the website?"

Reviewing those statistics is as basic and requisite as glancing at the instrument panel of your auto as you drive. Site performance reviews are a requisite monthly or bi-monthly action item for your law firm's marketing agenda.

If you don't have analytics on your site, get them. Google Analytics, the industry standard, is free. ◆

What Do the Jurors Think of Your Website?

Most law firms carefully craft their websites to leave a certain impression with potential clients, the firm's existing clients, referral sources, employees and potential employees.

Have you ever considered what sitting jurors might think of your litigators and firm after a visit to your website during trial?

Jury consultants lecturing at national conventions confirm what interviews of jurors in trials consistently tell our clients. Most jurors tour your firm's website and read about you and your colleagues, your work and your firm. And, they do it during voir dire and during trial, despite admonishments from the bench.

So your firm's commitments to the community, pro bono projects, the way you explain and present yourself and how you portray your past successes for people and businesses are being routinely investigated by those sitting in the box.

Defense counsel may want to soften their image of being Goliath's hired guns. Plaintiff's counsel may want to position themselves as champions of the Davids of the world. Many personal injury and family law firms explain their involvement in Arrive Alive, domestic violence prevention, scholarship and underage drinking programs on their websites already. They have fan pages and testimonials on social media sites to humanize them.

Whatever you convey on your site should be consistent with the impression you are trying to make to jurors in the courtroom. ◆

How to Manage Your Online Reputation

Online advice and recommendations are as important as personal word-of-mouth referrals, a new study from Cone, one of the world's largest ad agencies, shows. The former can derail the latter because most people rely upon online information as confirmation before retaining a lawyer.

Here's what we recommend attorneys do to properly manage their online reputation.

Corporate, transactional and defense lawyers should:

- Have full Martindale-Hubbell listings and obtain an AV rating
- Get nominated and try to be voted a Super Lawyer® or Rising Star®
- Try to be nominated and voted to *Best Lawyers*®, and if you make it, buy a link on their site
- Be on LinkedIn, and seek Connections with clients (where appropriate) and with other professionals and lawyers, and ask for recommendations (if local bar rules allow testimonials)
- Claim and update your AVVO profile
- Make sure profiles on directories managed by institutes, colleges or academies are up-to-date

Lawyers targeting consumers (PI, divorce and personal bankruptcy for example) should do the same. One major consideration for those targeting consumers is the value of a listing and rating in Martindale. We recommend you have a full Martindale listing and obtain an AV rating if lawyer referrals are an important component of your personal business development.

Independent studies are coming in on a regular basis now so this list is likely to evolve quickly. As of this writing, what data there is indicates the above efforts will be sufficient to confirm the hard work you put into getting word-of-mouth referrals. ◆

Study Shows Americans Spend More Time Online Than Watching Television: Lawyers Need to Consider Video

It is generally known that Americans now spend more time online than they do watching television. Less recognized is that 90 percent of the U.S. Internet audience viewed at least one online video last month and that 40 percent of all online adults sought out <u>educational</u> videos in the past 30 days.

Those statistics and others below clearly show there's an opportunity for your law practice to develop cases by shooting video and putting it on the Internet and your website.

That video will be a critical behind-the-scenes role in your case development. It will confirm word-of-mouth referrals. The reason: most prospects urged to contact you by third parties commonly go online to check out a lawyer and firm before making direct contact. The proof is a study by Cone, one of the largest advertising agencies in the world, which showed a majority of people confirm word-of-mouth referrals *for doctors, dentists, accountants and lawyers* by going online. If a professional's digital presence did not match what they had been told, Cone found 80 percent of people had ignored the personal recommendations they'd been given. Cone reported 90 percent followed through on a personal recommendation when a professional's online presence was consistent with what they'd been told.

Advertising agencies have always said there is nothing more powerful than a demonstration. Remember the Kitchen Magician? *"It slices. It dices."*

http://www.youtube.com/watch?v=cGVG9xLHb84

Remember when they cut a piece of lead pipe with a Ginsu knife?

http://www.youtube.com/watch?v=4q7GCuWFsSs

American Lawyer Media (ALM) clearly weren't thinking of Ron Popeil and these iconic advertisements when they surveyed 300 in-house counsels last year. But they learned something Popiel knew long ago—to harness the power and memorability of a video demonstration. ALM learned in-house lawyers felt overwhelmingly that a video of a lawyer on a bio page was universally helpful. It allowed them to judge a practitioner's demeanor and professionalism in advance of contact. If you have a presence that can be shown on camera the same way it shows in person, you've got an advantage to seize online in video.

When creating a video, remember that what you say should not be about you but about the client's issues.

It's best to focus on issues that affect your potential client's daily decisions. Divorce attorney Lee Rosen has had more than 110,000 visits to this video:

http://www.youtube.com/watch?v=p9D7eTLZn8I.

Other videos he's posted have more than 150,000 views. That's right. One of his videos has been watched 150,000 times in just a few years. This video is one of a series of highly-instructional videos Rosen told me hundreds of prospects have said they viewed before contacting him.

This is the wrong way to do it:

http://www.youtube.com/watch?v=7zR6RX86ZUk.

Rosen gets 30 times the traffic of this lawyer and has great comments below his videos. This law firm hasn't had a comment in three years and the last one says "I did some research about some of the top law firms and came up with this helpful list you might want to take a look at if you need a lawyer." Ouch.

Videos aren't just for lawyers who deal with personal legal issues. Business attorney Ed Alexander in Orlando has created a successful YouTube Channel with numerous practical videos.

http://www.youtube.com/user/AttorneyEdAlexander/videos

A lawyer at Foley Lardner explains intellectual property issues manufacturers must consider in this video:

http://youtu.be/bP5ogSRrSqw

Rosen has a soundproof studio he built in his offices. Alexander is more informal. The style is up to you but I would recommend you hire a professional and save the cost Rosen went through to obtain the quality. For a few thousand dollars you can get a videographer to come into your offices, shoot for half a day, edit, professionally finish, create the YouTube channel and post a series of videos. You can have your webmaster embed the YouTube channel in your site and specific videos on the pages you want.

Not everyone can do videos unrehearsed. You may want to write scripts in advance and practice them. You don't need to buy teleprompter software if you want to read from a script. Use Word and have the script roll on a laptop. Control the speed at which you read yourself using a wireless mouse. Here's a video *(what else did you expect?)* of how to do it:

http://www.dailymotion.com/video/xhm5qc_creating-a-teleprompter
-with-microsoft-word_tech#.US_leTCG308.

Academic research also suggests that the online video revolution is an opportunity to make a better impression and increase your chances of being retained. Hee Jun Choi and Scott D. Johnson of the University of Illinois at Urbana-Champaign wrote in *The American Journal of Distance Education* that "... there is a significant difference in learners' motivation in terms of attention between the video-based instruction and traditional text-based instruction. In addition, the learners reported that the video-based instruction was more memorable than the traditional text-based instruction."

So forget that (text-based) brochure and the detailed practice area descriptions on your website.

The final question is one we get asked all the time: "How long should my marketing video be?"

There is no single correct answer, but there is a basic logic formula to follow. The length of your video is directly related to the expectation of the viewer, the experts say.

"A non-technical analogy would be a billboard on a freeway. It needs to communicate a clear and powerful message in just the few seconds the driver can look at it while driving by at 70mph. On the other hand, if I ask someone for more information about what they are selling, I'm willing to spend more time reading it," says Vipe, a video marketing cloud-based software provider focusing on B2B organizations.

Research by Vipe reveals that 54 percent of viewers stop watching an educational video after 60 seconds. Just 23 percent are still watching after two minutes. It's hard to say much in 30 seconds but one third of those watching drop away at that point. ◆

Study Shows Weak Online Profiles
Thwart Word of Mouth Recommendations

Research has long shown nothing is more powerful than a word-of-mouth recommendation from a trusted source, but a new study shows failing to fully back it up by properly managing your online reputation will quickly subvert the hard work you invested to get someone to pass your name along.

In other words, due to the near-universal reach and acceptance of the Internet, online recommendations are now approaching equality in importance with offline advice.

So says the international ad agency Cone in its Online Influence Trend Tracker report: "Our latest research reveals four-out-of-five consumers have changed their minds about purchasing a recommended product or service based solely on negative information they found online."

That's up from 67 percent of consumers in 2010, according to Cone, one of the oldest and most respected advertising, public relations and strategic branding agencies. And, it's consistent with what we see in our own law firm marketing surveys and hear when interviewing law firm clients, both business executives and in-house counsel, about how they vet lawyers.

"Online information, a trustworthy source for 89 percent of consumers, has the power to make or break a recommendation," Cone reported.

That backs up what recent surveys, one of more than 500 in-house lawyers, have revealed about how lawyers can best market their practices. Failing to have listings and having no or a weaker rating in databases such as Martindale-Hubbell, Super Lawyers, AVVO, or having no presence on, say, LinkedIn, all serve to make retention unlikely, said house counsel in recent landmark surveys conducted by BTI Consulting and American Lawyer Media.

"Personal recommendations are just not enough," said the Cone report. "The explosion of online word-of-mouth channels and the adoption of online verification have forever changed the marketing landscape."

Chapter 8:

Rainmaking, Client Service Basics and Referrals

— ◆ —

Value of Non-traditional Marketing Roles

It is unreasonable to expect every lawyer in your firm to market in the same traditional way—acting as a "hunter" and attending events, serving on committees, making speeches, fundraising and teaching continuing professional education.

But that does not mean every lawyer in your firm cannot contribute significantly to business development.

All lawyers can contribute to a law firm's marketing in a way that is comfortable to them. Attorney and marketing consultant Stacy West Clark describes this as finding "critically important behind-the-scenes roles" for partners and associates who are unwilling or uncomfortable marketing publicly. As we all know, many lawyers are disinterested in developing a book of their own business. They do best on accounts developed by others, maximizing opportunities to serve existing needs and identifying cross-selling opportunities.

What can those "service" lawyers do?

- Write articles, blog posts, speeches, seminar presentations
- Develop prospect databases and contact schedules for working through them
- Evaluate trade and community groups and activity within each
- Monitor, evaluate and update your website
- Monitor competitors' marketing
- Update and manage client and referral lists

These are critical contributions to marketing.

Of course, like the efforts of the traditional rainmaker these "behind-the-scenes" efforts by your less public lawyers needs to recognized in your compensation plan. ◆

Rainmaking: Another Study Reveals How Much Time You Should Spend

The landmark 2003 study of women rainmakers—the first definitive report tabulating how much time lawyers spent to create a solid book of business—was updated a few years ago and reconfirmed the finding of the original report. As well, in February 2014 yet another study was released confirming the time investment required to become a "rainmaker" is the same no matter your gender.

Based on 400 interviews, the two studies of women rainmakers by the Legal Sales and Services Organization (LSSO) indicated the threshold for success is for lawyers to devote eight hours weekly to personal business development. Spend less than eight hours and originations plummet.

Those women lawyers who spent eight hours weekly on marketing had annual origination of $472,000. Ten hours on average spent weekly equaled $590,000 in annual originations, according to the LSSO surveys.

Confirming the time commitment needed Lawyer Metrics, a group of statisticians, I/O psychologists, and lawyers, has just released its Rainmaker Study. It was based on performance data from over 300 partners primarily at AmLaw 100 and AmLaw 200 firms. It revealed that rainmakers average about 465 hours per year on client development (that's 8.9 hours weekly) whereas client service partners average about 325 hours per year (that's 6.25 hours weekly).

Of course, as we often discover when writing law firm marketing plans and coaching lawyers, the vast majority, male or female, just don't make the needed time commitment. On average, our surveys reveal most lawyers spend just 3-4 weekly on business development. The LSSO report reveals what activities successful business developers engage in that less successful business generators tend to avoid—joining business groups, leading those groups, speaking and asking clients for work and referrals to others who may need their services. That those are the highest-yielding tactics is confirmed by our biannual National Marketing Effectiveness Survey.

The final clause of the last sentence bears repetition: top rainmakers ask for work and for referrals from their clients and prospects. Asking for work, in a professional manner at the correct time after establishing trust and enthusiasm, is a critical sales skill most lawyers fail to develop. ◆

What Do Rainmakers Do That Less Successful Lawyers Don't?

Our anecdotal observations in law firms over the past two decades about what differentiates top rainmakers who generate enough work to keep themselves and associates busy from lawyers who struggle to generate enough business to fill just their own plate every year have been confirmed by a national survey.

In short, the rainmakers "speak, join and party."

And, one-third of those rainmakers devote an average of 15 hours or more every month to those activities while another 20 percent devote 11 to 14 hours.

The survey, first done in 2003 and then confirmed five years later, was conducted by the Legal Sales and Service Organization (LSSO) and included 400 women lawyers who were split into two groups for comparison. Our observation is that the survey results are equally applicable to men. The rainmakers in the original survey dubbed "very successful" averaged about $800,000 of annual originations while the so-called "less successful" group averaged $327,000 of originations.

While both rainmakers and less successful lawyers were active in bar associations, community and trade associations, the very successful were far more likely to take leadership roles both there and in nonprofits, in which 70 percent reported also being active. This was true whether the lawyers reported the activity was designed primarily to seek new clients or establish referral sources.

We have long counseled our attorneys to take leadership roles in the groups in which they are active. Simply attending events is not enough. A board position or serving as a committee chair allows/forces lawyers to seek out other members and create working relationships. In the process, they demonstrate the qualities that prompt others to recommend or hire them.

Equally telling in the survey results was that the top rainmakers demonstrated twice the propensity for public speaking over their less successful counterparts. Interestingly, the comparatively passive tactic of publishing ranked lower as a business development tool for both groups.

Finally, top rainmakers were two to three times more likely to network and ask clients and referral sources for introductions to others. That's no surprise. The most successful salespeople have always been those who manage to comfortably and seamlessly "ask for the order." ◆

Former Court Clerks, PDs and Prosecutors Have Built-in Alumni Networks

Many associates who began their legal careers as court clerks, public defenders or prosecutors are now trying to build referral networks so they can make partner. Other associates in your firm may have attended law schools in states other than that in which they are now practicing. These situations provide alumni marketing opportunities that many firms ignore.

Court clerks can organize a clerk alumni network and hold a reception or series of presentations at your firm. (The reunions of U.S. Supreme Court clerks in Washington are legendary.) Those events can be more than just reunions for the sake of networking. They might include presentations or appearances by judges from the court where the associates served or feature speakers on professional development issues. After organizing the first such event, your lawyers might put together an alumni directory so everyone can stay in touch. The same is true for PDs and prosecutors.

Associates who attended law schools in faraway cities or states can organize alumni groups too. We've had clients who invited the deans and professors from their law schools to attend alumni gatherings. The dean needs alumni support to help attract students and place future graduates.

So often the best marketing contacts attorneys can make are with those people they once knew well but with whom they have allowed their relationships to fade over time. What alumni groups is your firm unaware it might organize? ◆

The Single Most Difficult
and Valuable Marketing Tactic

We are often asked what is the single most difficult marketing problem facing local and regional law firms. Our answer: database development and management.

What we mean by this is simple—most law firms do not have a reliable and updated system of managing client and other contact information. Software companies call it "client relationship management" or a CRM program. More simply put, it's your mailing list. (Just how much fun is it in your firm when it comes time to deal with the holiday card and gift list?)

If lawyers were as diligent organizing and managing the contact information for their clients and referral sources as they are about the documents for their cases, they would not have a problem. But when it comes to capturing essential marketing information, as a general rule, most law firms are sloppy. A law firm's single most valuable asset—aside from their expertise practicing law—is its client and referral source list, and for most firms it's scattered about, out-of-date and missing key information.

This is a critical problem for which each law firm must find a solution. When we work with law firms to develop a marketing plan, we typically start with a client survey. What we have found in surveying about 5,000 clients from dozens of law firms across the country in recent years is that, almost without exception, law firm clients say they want emailed updates from their lawyers, the lawyers they trust most, about the law and how it will affect their personal and business decisions. Based on this, any lawyer or law firm who thinks their clients do not want this kind of communication is wrong. (This is true of tort practices, too. Clients universally want personal safety information so they can protect their families from accidents. Referring lawyers say they want it too.)

And, frankly, it's bad business not to provide such information. No one disagrees with Dale Carnegie who said, "Tell the audience what you're going to say, say it; then tell them what you've said." The only way a law firm can accomplish that kind of frequency of communication with its client and re-ferral source base is if they have an organized and updated database.

If what the clients say they want isn't enough to motivate a business law firm to solve this issue then consider this: studies of billions of dollars of approved corporate legal invoice indicate regular legal updates like we are describing also translate into higher hourly billing rates. In other words, the better your mailing list, the better your database, the more valuable your services are considered and the more you can charge. For plaintiffs firms, the frequency of communication that becomes possible translates into top-mind-awareness over time. In other words, you get the call and you get the referral, rather than the TV or online advertiser.

Here are some steps we recommend to tame the database monster at your firm:

1. Change firm culture

The major roadblock to effective database management is changing familiar behavior. The firms that experience the most success with this are those that sit down as a group and agree they are going to prioritize this at the firm. Hopefully, lawyers will begin to form a habit that the people they meet (clients, potential clients and referral sources) end up in the database. If lawyers are not able to do this, then the firm must establish processes for others to do so. Everyone must be fully informed about why the database is important and trained to ask the right questions. Who did you have lunch with today? Should they get alerts or the firm newsletter? What about a holiday card?

2. Identify a task force of three to five people from the firm to lead the database development/clean-up and management process

In order for this effort to be successful, it must have buy-in throughout the firm. The best way to achieve that is for a small group to research software options and lead the process for the entire firm. Using internal law firm representatives, rather than simply an outside consultant, will increase your ability to create firm-wide buy-in.

3. See if your current case management/time and billing system has a reasonably priced marketing module available

In the early 1990s, hand written time logs and basic document management systems started becoming a thing of the past with the advent of electronic time keeping and billing. Unfortunately, it didn't occur to most vendors at the time that those software systems should have a marketing component as well. About a decade later, many of those companies did develop marketing modules to add on to the existing systems but they came at a premium price. Those modules, at a more reasonable price, are now available for some systems and might be the right answer for your firm. Investigate that option before turning to other CRM software systems. (We are familiar with a number of CRM software systems—call us to learn more.)

4. Research Outlook-based systems, or if you use Macs check into Daylite

Now, there is a generation of software companies with names including IntelliPad® and ContactEase® that use Microsoft Outlook® as a foundation. These can be reasonably priced, user-friendly options for many law firms. Recently, we have worked with firms in the Apple world that successfully employs Daylite as their CRM in conjunction with iMail.

5. Evaluate the options, including installation and ongoing support

The single most important criteria for any database management system your law firm adopts is this: Is it easy for people to use? Get some references from other firms about the software vendor's performance during installation and in providing subsequent support.

6. Develop a process that will ensure information is entered, updated and purged on a regular basis

It takes months to demonstrate, evaluate and then fully install a new CRM system. Many firms just avoid the issue because of this required investment. Once in place, however, the job is not done. A database is only effective if updated information is entered and outdated information is purged on a regular basis.

7. Use the database

Now that your firm has this valuable tool, you have to use it. Send single topic alerts—information affecting the client's day-to-day decision-making—on a regular basis. Compile your best-read alerts (you should be using CANSPAM compliant software that shows your open rates, among other metrics) into an emailed newsletter sent quarterly to clients and referral sources, adding in a dose of firm news to support credibility (think awards, hiring announcements, key rulings, verdicts, settlements or retentions.) Generating content should not be a problem. Every day in emails, letters, phone calls, briefs, and CLE/CPE presentations, lawyers are giving advice that can be repurposed as helpful articles for a general client audience and for referral sources.

Here's a specific example of what we mean. We received a wonderfully detailed and informative letter recently from our IP lawyer about our newly-registered trademark "Alyn-Weiss' Monthly Marketing Brief®." Within that letter was guidance that could be slightly rewritten and used as numerous blog posts on the law firm's website. We think the lawyer could modify various portions of his letter to us to create two or more "client alerts." These could be written alerts or sent as emails. He could send these alerts over time directly to all of the firm's business clients so they understand issues related to fully protecting their marks. From a single letter advising us he can generate content that may get him work from online search, from other lawyers who don't handle IP or from other clients of the firm.

Do we mind that a letter he charged our company for (which probably contains information used before in his other letters but was customized for our trademark and our business) is subsequently modified and used this way? Absolutely not. The lawyer's understanding of our business, his forethought and diligence and responsiveness, and his demonstrated expertise with IP, in other words, his overall relationship with us, is why we retain him. We know that what he advises us to do, he also advises others in similar situations to do.

Firms that have addressed the database as we describe above have never looked back on the time and money spent as not worth the investment. When firms implement a database system, we quickly hear "We got a case" following an alert being sent. This is not an expense but a capital investment. And, the near immediate response and increase in revenue once the database problem is harnessed makes it all worthwhile. ◆

You Can't Tell Who's Playing Without a Program— Know Your Lateral Hires

"You can't tell who's playing without a program" the barkers call just inside the gates of the stadium. They were yelling the same thing 40 years ago when I attended my first Major League Baseball game, and they continue to yell it today.

Fans don't question the need for a program when there is value to quickly familiarizing themselves with the names and capabilities of players.

So do you give your newest fans—your lateral hires and new associates—a program of the players when they step inside the gates of your firm for the first time?

"To get comfortable, to fit in here, I need to know what everyone does, in terms of their practice areas and important cases," said a lateral shareholder who recently joined a 60-lawyer firm. "And a picture of everyone on a sheet of paper, having names on lawyer's office doors and on legal assistant and paralegal desks would be really helpful."

She's right. And, the pictures are essential. They're like numbers on uniforms. They quickly identify the players and their positions.

"The firm website is just too cumbersome and slow to use," another lateral recently told me. And it's difficult to study a website designed with other goals in mind.

We all know that many lateral hires fail to stick at firms. Most associates are gone within a few years.

Hiring failures are a tremendous disappointment and costly to everyone involved, including clients. Easing the integration of laterals and associates into the firm only improves your chances of retaining lawyers you want to keep. Give them a program. ◆

What Callers Hear When They Are Put on Hold

What do prospects and clients "hear" when they call your firm and are put on hold?

It's not something lawyers think about much but research shows a small investment can buy you a lot of time. And since most callers are put on hold, at least briefly, what happens as they wait is critical to your firm's business.

Nearly 90 percent of callers report they hang up after being on silent hold for 40 seconds, according to *AT&T and Telecommunication Magazine*. That's important because the average time callers spend on hold at businesses with more than two lines is 55 seconds, according to one regional phone company.

Most callers say they hang up because they begin to wonder if their call has become inadvertently lost. It's generally agreed that prospective clients will not call back, particularly if they have another lawyer's name on a list of several to whom they have been referred. Clients will try again but that just doubles your receptionist's workload and causes unneeded frustration.

If you play music into your phone system your callers will hang on for another 30 seconds before disconnecting, the studies say.

If you invest in a tape or CD that describes your firm's work, community support and history, or which provides legal tips, you can keep someone on hold for nearly three minutes without them hanging up or noticing much of a delay.

Of course, your standard of practice shouldn't be to keep anyone waiting on hold for three minutes. At the same time and despite the advent of e-mail, most firms still experience periods of high call volume. Putting some callers on hold is simply inevitable at a successful law firm.

Investing in a prerecorded custom message will ensure your callers stay around to hear you out. And, providers are easy to find on the Internet. ◆

The Perfect Reception Area—
From a Marketing Standpoint

In real estate, they call it "curb appeal," the critical first impression a property, residential or commercial, makes when a buyer or potential tenant first arrives.

What sort of impression about your firm does your lobby make to the first-time visitor? A lobby with a copy of today's local paper and a tattered weekly news magazine is a missed marketing opportunity.

One firm we represent that works with rapidly growing high-technology firms has big-screen televisions on the wall running news and financial programming, "We're apace and connected to the capital markets" is the message they convey to clients.

A firm with multinational clients has the day's International Herald Tribune and Financial Times on the coffee table, and a TV on which CNN's international news broadcasts run. "We're connected to the world and are up-to-date on events affecting your operations" is the clear message.

A regional firm we represent has pictures of manufacturing and distribution facilities of clients on the wall. Each has a short explanation of the client's business and the nature of the firm's representation. (Discreetly on the bottom of each it says, "This display developed with the permission of our client.")

Yet another firm profiles a major client each quarter in its lobby, inviting the client's PR people to help the firm's marketing director develop a display of products, facilities and history. This has the added benefit of educating the firm's lawyers and staff about the client base and services the firm provides.

Other firms create displays of client annual reports or product catalogs, again with the client's permission, for visitors to see. (Each publication says on a label in the corner—"We are proud to represent ABC Inc., providing such and such services. This display was developed with the permission of our client.")

Retailers have long had lobby and showroom displays of their advertisements. "As seen in Big City Magazine," the headline says over a copy of their ad. Displaying copies of current advertising is appropriate in a law firm office lobby as well. Copies of your recent professional announcements also should be on display, along with news releases and clippings in which the firm's lawyers are quoted, and your most recent newsletter, client guides, and alerts. Some firms organize scrapbooks and include pictures of firm charitable events.

What does your lobby say about your firm and what it can do for clients? ◈

Common Reasons Lawyers Over Age 50 Lose Clients

On a regular basis, I meet attorneys in their mid-50s who tell me their compensation has dropped because they no longer originate business as they once did. Some have been de-equitized from their partnerships.

They tell me that their business owner clients have sold out or that the owner transitioned the management of a closely-held company to a son or daughter. Others explain that the in-house counsel they have worked with for years retired or moved up in the client organization and a new associate general counsel now manages case assignments.

Those who replaced their key contacts and referral sources "wanted a lawyer their age," they say. Universally, these lawyers with declining books of business don't look at what they may have done to actively contribute to their situation.

When I meet these lawyers, there are obvious commonalities. When I interview their former clients and former referral sources I learn "wanting a lawyer their own age" was not the primary reason for the change in counsel. Clients and referral sources instead say the reason they changed counsel was because the older lawyers gradually indicated they were not as competent, despite their experience, or were not as motivated about the practice of law as the younger lawyers selected to replace them.

Specifically, I see the following characteristics in veteran, usually over the age of 50, lawyers who report their practices are in decline.

- They have quit attending functions or meetings of key trade groups where their clients and referral sources gather.
- They (too) often say, "I've been practicing 30 years and my experience is..." This is obvious. Clients and referral sources tell me they find such statements irrelevant, even annoying. Some say it indicates their lawyer isn't open to new ideas.
- Many still prefer the phone to email. They are slow responding to e-mail. They don't text. They complain about and struggle with technology. Many still dictate *(shudder!)*. The phone has a dimin-

ished role in business. Today 80+ percent of business communication is by e-mail.

- Many have dated wardrobes and hair. They don't own a single pair of plain front pants. Their glasses are many years out of style. They overdress.
- Many are physically out-of-shape and do not project vitality and enthusiasm.*
- Many are not active on social media and lack a presence there which "hinders" retention, according to recent surveys.

Non-lawyers base the selection of counsel on anecdotal evidence. Since they aren't lawyers, relying on non-legal factors in the selection process is all they have. What is revealing is that other lawyers rely on those factors, too. Experience counts—it's your competitive edge. Survey after survey shows that the two most important factors in selecting counsel are a familiarity with the legal issue at hand and knowledge of an industry. Veteran lawyers who avoid the pitfalls described above will out-compete (younger lawyers) and maintain control of their file flow and rate. ◆

*Want to change your life? Read *Younger Next Year*, a *New York Times* bestseller.

Losing a Senior or Key Lawyer— Steps to Take in the Event of Them Being Recruited Away, Death or an Untimely Disability

I recently wrote about best practices when a veteran lawyer joins your firm, a post prompting one reader to ask what is best when one departs. We have dealt several times with the loss of founders and name partners to competitors and to the bench. Sadly, several times in recent years we have found ourselves handling the sudden death or disability of name and managing partners as well.

Lateral recruiting is now the preferred growth strategy of most firms, so ultimately most firms will face these situations.

Of course, a partner who goes to the bench is cause for celebration. A loss to a competing firm of a key timekeeper and business generator tends to come as a surprise and is often seen as threatening the organization's financial stability. In the case of a death clear-thinking—under the duress of grief—while compassionately but prudently settling the estate is emotionally confusing and draining.

In the case of losing a partner to the bench congratulations are in order, including a reception after the swearing in. Issue discreet written and email invitations consistent with your local bar customs. Your partner's new colleagues on the bench can explain what's customary for your soon-to-be-judge. If a name partner goes to the bench, you'll have to change the name of your entity. That means you get a chance to email and place ads announcing your firm's new name. It also lets you remind everyone who at your firm still practices the kind of law your former partner handled. Make sure you identify your former partner's key referral sources and any trade and community groups in which she was active. Get your next generation educated, introduced and involved in and with all ASAP. Most lawyers let their partners know well in advance when the politics are right and they are going to apply for a judgeship, so this is something you can work on sooner than later.

Death or disability is a personal wound to an organization, whether sudden or anticipated, whether due to accident or disease. Every situation is different. Think first about the clients, who—while polite—will rightly consider their own interests first. Get word to them as fast as you can and get right to the point if you want to keep them. It's likely you'll keep current matters. It's the next matter you need to be concerned about. Think second about your lawyers and keeping them. Only then talk to your staff, which while polite, will be considering their own interests first too. Do not make an announcement on any list serv, or to any legal or other media until you must.

Ethically, we all know advertising materials must be truthful, so all website pages, directories, letterhead and other promotional materials must be changed ASAP. Coffee mugs and branded coasters lingering in conference rooms with deceased lawyer names on them have proved embarrassing to firms. On your site, placing a black border on the lawyer's profile page with a note saying the lawyer passed away on a certain date and that referrals, ongoing case inquiries and other questions are being handled by lawyer(s) whose direct dials and emails are listed there has worked well for our clients. We recommend our client firms keep the bios on the site in this form for 13 months before taking the page down—veteran rainmakers will receive referrals many months after death or disability in our experience. Keep the lawyer's email address active and have it forward to another professional. Change LinkedIn to reflect the situation and monitor communications there for six months before closing the account. Update Martindale, Best Lawyers and other online directories, including those of colleges and academies.

Losing a veteran partner to a competitor when you want to keep some of their work creates all manner of difficulty. We recommend you take the high road and be as transparent as possible—you'll retain the maximum amount of work by doing so. Some firms will openly congratulate their former partner in an announcement in their bar journal saying they wish them well.

Clients who transfer active files to your former partner's new firm may not stay at the new firm. Our experience is that some of those clients will send their next or future matters to you. New firms with new billing practices and a different rate structure create unexpected opportunities. What's requisite is telling the former client you'd like their future work. And doing that in person is key albeit uncomfortable for many lawyers. If they aren't going to send you any work, they'll tell you up front when you call. You have not lost anything by trying. ◆

Consistent Presentation of Your Firm Name and Logo Is More Important Than You Think

Imagine that you are driving on an interstate and have become hungry and decided to eat. Just above the top of a stand of trees ahead you catch a glimpse of the corner of a golden arch.

That sliver of a (worldwide trademarked) symbol immediately triggers reactions and thoughts in light of your situation. Those reactions and thoughts are proof of the incredible value of using graphics that are consistent and employed across different media—in this case, on bags, cups, signage, TV, billboards, napkins, sandwich wrappers. This is something most law firms fail to understand.

The golden arches cause you to consider your diet, how much money you have in your pocket, how much time you have to spend eating, prior experiences with the provider and its competition, etc.

Your thought process, and whether you turned off to go to McDonald's, would have been different had you instead seen one of those blue highway signs on the shoulder of the road depicting a knife and fork and saying "Next Exit," or just a big sign in front of a nondescript building saying "Fine Food."

Every law firm needs to invest in a consistent presentation of its image. This is particularly important for corporate, transactional and defense groups. They have fewer chances than consumer product companies or, say, advertising plaintiff lawyers, to touch their target market. Relentlessly consistent graphic presentation of your firm's name reinforces the good feelings of your clients and encourages referrals because it triggers memories of prior experience and the quality of your work. Recognize the key to building recognition of a mark like the golden arches lies in years of near-perfect execution.

Where law firms need to be careful:

- Never vary how your firm name appears. Not sometimes on one line and sometimes on two; not at the top of the page and then at the bottom; not differently because of limited space in an advertisement or because "it's just my church bulletin."

- Keep your logo and all your stationery, including business cards and presentation materials (announcements, lobby signage, conference room coasters, PowerPoint slides, blogs, website, handouts, invitations and advertisements) printed in the same colors. Write down these standards; rigorously enforce them on every item distributed by the firm. (Yes, we see older partners at some firms resist conformity—we can also tell you, universally, that those firms are less profitable than average.)

- Make sure the graphics in your e-mail signature block match as well. Carry that over to schwag too.

  Develop or find a truly distinctive picture or mark, call it a logo, if you like (think of Texaco's star, Target's, well, red target). Don't use the scales of justice, a gavel, columns of any type, chess pieces, law books or a skyline unless you serve out-of-state clients and it's somehow distinctive and important to the services they are likely to need.

  Avoid the first letters of your partners' names hooked together in a circle or square. Hundreds of firms use these predictable treatments; I guarantee several in your city do. This stuff is the knife and fork sign of the legal world.

Does this constitute a measure of what is called "branding," meaning it differentiates, is enduring and makes a difference to those who see it? Yes, albeit to a very limited degree and at limited expense. It's a start. ◆

In a Beauty Contest to Win Business, Is It Best to Present First, in the Middle or Last?

If you were one of three lawyers or firms in a beauty contest would you want to present first, second or last?

This is an increasingly important question. General counsel and executives in bet-the-company situations and consumers facing the consequences of high-asset divorce or catastrophic injury, more often than not are interviewing more than one lawyer or firm. Our surveys and anecdotal information indicate that clients no longer base retention simply on reputation or a colleague's referral.

So, we asked about 125 veteran attorneys the question about order of presentation and why they believed their strategy worked best.

The overall answer: 52 percent preferred going third, 48 percent wanted to present first. None wanted to be in the middle. There was a difference, however, in the view of litigators and transactional lawyers.

By a factor of four, the business/transactional lawyers said they preferred going third. The litigators also preferred going third, but the margin was razor-thin—51 percent to 49 percent.

The lawyers we quizzed advised major corporations on governance, securities and pension funds, major banks and real estate companies on the development side. Several were defense counsel to Fortune 500 companies. Several had traditional high-end personal injury practices. A few also filed business torts on the plaintiff side.

A few who wanted to go first felt they could stop the process and close the deal before others were even interviewed. Others reported they had learned to go third the hard way—by going first when given a choice. Some cited theory, "primacy" and "recency" were mentioned. More than one argued that going first allowed the bar to be set high, and if other presenters did not reach it, "absence" would result in a win. Others felt potential clients learned what they really wanted during the interview process. Going last meant the prospect could be asked what had emerged during the first two interviews as most important and the presentation could be modified accordingly to win the engagement.

In the end, there is consensus about one thing—you want to stay out of the middle. ◆

Should You Cut Your Marketing Expenses in a Recession?

Many firms trimmed their marketing budgets in reaction to the Great Recession. Is there any data firms can use to guide budgeting during an economic downturn? (One has to come again.)

Yes. We have located studies from every recession going back to the 1920's. They discuss the risks and rewards of budget cutbacks and expansions during a recession. They are from respected sources: the Harvard Business Review and McGraw Hill among others.

All show the same results—business-to-business firms that maintained or increased their advertising expenditures during recessions over the past 90 years have averaged significantly higher sales growth, both during the recession and for the following three years, than those that eliminated or decreased advertising. In the three years following the 1980-1981 recession, revenues of companies that were aggressive recession advertisers rose 256 percent over those that didn't keep up their advertising, according to McGraw Hill.

The studies track performance of major advertisers of business-to-business products and services. We have not been able to locate a study of professional services firms possibly because lawyers, architects, CPAs, engineers and health care providers were not permitted to advertise and otherwise market until 1980.

These are links and sites of studies and white papers:

- http://www.jimcoxassociates.com:16080/marketing411/articles /a_recession_can_be_good.pdf

- http://hbswk.hbs.edu/item/5878.html

- Study conducted by Roland S. Vaile and published in the Harvard Business Review, April, 1927

- Study conducted by Buchen Advertising, Inc., 1949, 1954, 1958 and 1961 recessions

- Meldrum & Fewsmith, Inc., the American Business Press, 1970

- McGraw-Hill Research, Laboratory of Advertising Performance Report 5262 New York: McGraw-Hill, 1986

- Billett Consultancy and Taylor Nelson AGB: The Billett/AGB Report 1993

- "Options and Opportunities for Consumer Businesses: Advertising During a Recession"

- The Center for Research & Development, October 1990

- Garbett, Thomas, How to Build a Corporation's Identity and Project Its Image.

- Lexington Books, D.C., Heath and Company, 1988

- DDB Needham Worldwide, "Advertising in Recessionary Times," October 8, 1990

We cannot locate one paper, book or speech made in opposition to these views. ◆

Marketing Spending Rebounds Post-recession and Online Promotion Now Creates a Flow of Lucrative New Matters for Business Law Firms

Legal marketing spending has rebounded to pre-recession levels according to our 2014 national survey of local and regional business law firms.

Another key finding in the survey in which we sought to determine what marketing tactics work best and which are in decline in addition to spending patterns: law practices must effectively embrace digital promotion or they will miss being considered for desirable cases they are qualified to handle. For some firms, those cases developed online are the single largest matters firms report developing this year.

On average firms reported having spent 3.4 percent of their annual collected fees on marketing and business development activities in 2014. Our National Marketing Effectiveness Survey included responses from 117 local and regional law firms and was completed this fall. All responding firms practiced corporate, transactional and defense litigation and the average size firm had 37 lawyers.

Coming out of the recession in 2012, firms had reported cutting spending to just 2.3 percent of annual fee volume on marketing. That was down from 3.4 percent in our 2010 survey, 2010 being the highest percentage spent on marketing we'd ever recorded.

The drop in 2012 was the first spending decline recorded by Alyn-Weiss since we started conducting our bi-annual survey of local and regional corporate, transactional and defense firms in 1990. In our initial 1990 survey firms reported spending just 1.45 percent of annual fees on marketing. Firms had gradually increased their marketing spending, even during the dot-com crash, until the Great Recession.

Our analysis of the latest survey results confirms that law firms which do not employ blogging, LinkedIn, effective websites, e-alerts, online rankings and ratings directories are simply missing out on desirable work.

The data concomitantly reaffirms that you can still be successful running a firm based solely on the traditional relationship tactics relied upon by firms for decades—the word-of-mouth promotional model that includes seminars, client entertainment, trade and community group presence. However, the data makes it equally clear that some work firms are receiving comes completely as a result of online rankings, online client reviews, LinkedIn, blogging and a firm's website. In fact, many of our clients report the single largest case they have right now has come from digital promotion. And, in the Midwest those cases all involve inheritance litigation, a development we predicted and trend we advise all firms in states with aging populations carefully consider.

The traditional law firm word-of-mouth marketing model has competition, or a companion, the online model. Employing a combination of the two is the most effective way to market a law practice, the survey reveals.

It bears repeating: for years we have said the practice of law has always been a personal relationship business and will always be a personal relationship business. The data now reveals highly profitable cases and files also come to firms whose new clients identify and fully vet them online absent a personal recommendation or relationship with your friend, colleague or other lawyer.

That firms can develop clients fully absent a referral or prior personal or professional relationship is a shift unsurprising to younger lawyers with whom we have reviewed the survey results. Millennials we coach understand this communication model works for a portion of the market, but it remains a leap of faith for many mid-career and senior practitioners.

A bio on your firm's website, after a law diploma, is a lawyer's most critical document the data shows. Websites are the single most effective tactic firms employ according to the survey. Asked what tactics have brought work to their firm directly and by referral over the past 18-24 months, 70 percent of the 117 firms in the survey said their website generated new matters.

The next most effective tactic was seminars/presentations which 51 percent of firms reported brought in cases, followed by law firm networks for 46 percent, trade and community groups 42 percent and entertainment for 31 percent of firms. Right behind those tactics came search engine optimization (coding of pages to ensure proper indexing), emailed alerts and newsletters, LinkedIn and blogging as being most effective.

The overall firm spending percentages do not include the cost of outside marketing consultants or in-house marketers. We ask firms to specifically exclude marketing personnel, agency and consulting fees because they vary so much from city to city compared to other "out-of-pocket" marketing expenses.

We surveyed firms of less than 100 lawyers because Alyn-Weiss needs to know what works and doesn't when it writes marketing plans, develops training and coaches lawyers at the firms they represent; those being firms competing directly with the AMLaw 250. Other questions asked in the survey include how firms govern their marketing programs, how effective firms find their marketing overall, what tactics firms expect to spend more or less time and money on in the coming year and if firms ask lawyers to record time spent on personal business development. ◆

What You Do After Making a Referral Is as Important as the Referral Itself

What occurs after you refer a matter to another lawyer or professional is as important as making the referral. The reason: you want to make sure the person you referred was well taken care of. If they weren't, this reflects poorly on you.

Our recommendations to maximize the value of a referral made include:

- Calling the person you referred soon after making the referral. Make sure the person's call was taken or that the e-mail sent or voice mail left was responded to in a timely fashion. Eventually, find out how well the matter was handled, if the results were satisfactory and if the fees charged were as estimated and fair.

- You should report on all of this back to the lawyer or professional to whom you made the referral. They'll appreciate it, even if part of what you report back is criticism. Of course, you should ask for permission to do this from the client and respect any request for confidentiality.

- We also recommend you refer to more than one provider at the outset. Consider giving three names. At any given time, the person to whom you are making a referral may decline the work. There are good reasons this can occur including they may be too busy to take on the matter, may have a conflict or may not mesh personally with the potential new client or assignment. Giving the person you are referring a choice, in terms of availability, temperament, fees and location, are important considerations. And, notify each provider that you have made the referral.

Referrals reflect directly on you. If handled with sensitivity and followed up on they will lead to reciprocation and goodwill. ◆

Do Clients and Referral Sources Really Care About Ethics? Study Shows No Matter What They Say About Ethical Behavior, Other Factors Are Most Important

We have always found it curious that while our lawyers list ethics, pro bono, community projects and in recent years green initiatives as important aspects of their marketing message, the law firm clients we survey never mention them as substantively affecting referrals and retention.

A new study shows why this may be the case.

We read this in Bulldog Reporter, a leading public relations service: "Eighty percent of consumers believe it is important for companies and brands to behave ethically—but the most significant factors when shopping are price, value and quality according to new research—from online sourcing and optimization specialists Trade Extensions—on UK and U.S. consumers' attitudes towards ethics and sustainability and how they affect purchasing decisions. The study suggests consumers display a 'do as I say, not as I do' attitude towards ethics and sustainability."

So, they conclude "It's critical to understand the differences between what people think—their attitudes—and what they actually do—their behavior..."

Clearly this report is sobering. Nonetheless, we think this is important data to consider when writing a law firm marketing plan, creating content and developing signature events. In short, don't lose sight of the need to always convey value and quality if you want a market response from your efforts. ◆

How Fast Should You Respond to Calls and E-Mails?

You should return clients calls and email on the same business day and within four hours.

That's the new standard we see in client satisfaction surveys we have completed over the past 12 months for both trial and transactional firms. We've asked: "What constitutes 'promptness' when receiving a response to your e-mails and phone calls?" More than 60 percent of clients say within "four hours." The "same business day" is the standard checked off about 30 percent of respondents and "within 24 hours" is the response for less than 10 percent of the more than 2,000 clients of law firms from which we have received responses in surveys we have completed.

What happens if you are in a deposition, a closing, hearing, a trial or are traveling? We decided to find that out and asked several dozen in-house counsel, executives and business owners. The answer: a response from an assistant or colleague will suffice.

It's not that you have to answer the caller's or sender's question or do anything immediately, we were told. Clients and referral sources just want acknowledgement their message has been received and the situation is set to be addressed within a reasonable timeframe. The same standard, we discovered in these interviews, goes for referrals—acknowledge the referral ASAP, contacting both the person who was referred and the person referring the matter to you.

What about inquiries made at 4:59 p.m.? That same evening is preferable to the next morning, but first thing in the morning is acceptable, our interviews indicated.

What about weekends? A response over the weekend is much appreciated but not considered requisite in most circumstances. ◆

A Personal Marketing Plan for Next Year in 15 Minutes

If you're too busy or disinclined to write a detailed personal marketing plan for the coming year, here's how you can build one using Microsoft Outlook in 15 minutes. List your top three clients and top three referral sources from the past 24 months.

These should be people who have the ability to send you desirable work from clients who pay. If you personally see the people you list regularly, more than quarterly in your normal activities, don't put them on this list. Our goal here is to establish frequency of contact, to keep those referrals coming. Also, do not list them if you currently have a regular flow of matters from them, and do not expect your last file from them to close in, say, the next six months.

Open "Tasks" in Outlook. List the six people and remind yourself to contact them by phone or email every 90 days for the next 12 months. The first time the names pop up this year, you will call each person. Tell them what matters you been involved in, ask them what is new with their business or practice, and how you might help them get more desirable work. Many lawyers say they find these conversations a bit awkward. If that's the case, call after hours and leave a voice mail. You'll be surprised how many people call you back. After all, they're your best contacts!

The second time the names come up send each person an e-mail. Keep it short. Topics might include a recent change in the law that could affect them or their clients or customers. Make sure it's relevant information somehow likely to affect their day-to-day business affairs.

Repeat the calls, voice mails and the e-mails on this schedule every 90 days.

Of course, I recommend you spend more time than this developing a strategy and tactics for the coming year. But busy lawyers are often disinclined to formalize their personal business development—at least until their book of business declines.

If you want to take a more formal approach to your personal marketing this coming year, there are a number of forms online from which to choose, some longer and more detailed than others. We have two-page forms for litigators, business lawyers and family law practitioner on our website you can download for free at www.themarketinggurus.com. ◆

Why Your Firm Should Send a Client Survey

Many law firms are uncomfortable doing client satisfaction surveys, a key step in writing a marketing plan. It often takes time to convince recalcitrant law firm partners that only good comes from asking clients how you can improve your firm and service. I mean "good" as in seeing increased referrals from clients that we can often track after a survey and "good" as in being assigned additional work soon after a survey of existing clients.

Here's a redacted email which general counsel of a Fortune 500 company sent to one of our clients recently. It was sent unsolicited after the in-house lawyer had completed an online client satisfaction survey we sent on the law firm's behalf:

"I just did the survey that was sent to me. While I was 'thinking' on the two of you, I wanted to make sure—if I hadn't already—that I told you how great I think you both are and what a wonderful job you did on the — —— litigation. I work with a lot of outside firms and can tell you that I was quite impressed with your team. So…thank you. And I hope we get the chance to work together in the future."

Receiving emails and personal comments like this is the rule, not the exception, when doing client surveys. ◆

How to Increase Your
Chances of Keeping a Client Sevenfold

Most firms do not spend much time focusing on cross-selling. It's the rare practice that actively seeks to expand the number of lawyers who are familiar with an account, no matter how many different practice groups work with that client. The statistics below, recently released on LexisNexis' blog Make More Rain, show why cross-selling should be a priority at your firm:

- When a law firm serves a client in just one area of law the risk of attrition is 35 percent; when a law firm serves a client in four or more areas of law the risk of attrition is less than five percent.
- When five or more law firm partners are involved with a client, fewer than 10 percent of those clients leave the law firm.

This data confirms why we recommend every law firm marketing plan include a formalized cross-selling strategy. We know cross-selling is not easy and not easy to stay focused upon, but it's critical to your long term success. It also saves you both time and money. It's well accepted that keeping clients costs less and is far easier than developing new ones.

The second statistic confirms what we had long suspected through anecdotal observation. It's now moved up on our list of 50+ best practices.

NOTE: We recognize many firms have objective compensation systems that do not incent cross-selling. Firms need to consider their compensation models if that's the case. ◆

An Effective Way to Market
a Boutique Litigation Practice

The most successful solo litigators and boutique litigation-only practices often get most of their cases from other lawyers. These include niche practices of one or just a few lawyers focused on plaintiff's personal injury, contingent-fee business (plaintiff) litigation, insurance recovery and, bad faith, commercial litigation, and criminal defense, including white-collar matters.

How do they reach other lawyers? Most teach continuing legal education to lawyers with whom they don't compete.

For example, personal injury lawyers from a large city, who limit their practice to wrongful death and catastrophic injury cases, teach basic PI law at suburban or rural county bar association meetings. They want the case the local general practitioner can't handle alone or can't fund.

Criminal lawyers teach corporate lawyers (at big firms or large in-house legal departments) how to advise clients when law enforcement arrives at the door with a subpoena. They also teach corporate lawyers to recognize when business activity begins to cross into the criminal realm. (Don't forget to mention your enthusiasm for traditional street crime misdemeanors and felonies!) They speak at local family bar meetings about how the courts are handling domestic violence.

Solo and small defense-only firms identify solo and small transactional-only firms in their market. They then meet with those potential referring lawyers and explain their experience, emphasizing the industries and legal issues with which they have dealt. It's your experience with particular legal issues and with an industry that makes the other lawyer's client comfortable hiring you (the same criteria general counsel report is most important when selecting outside counsel).

One final tip: aim to keep your presentations under one hour and make sure they qualify for CLE credit. ◆

Big Firm Lawyers Are Not Twice as Good, But Charge Twice as Much as Small Firms

Our clients, most of which are local and regional firms of 50 or so lawyers, regularly talk about the value their reduced billing rates present. However, they say they struggle to actually quantify and properly package the advantages when talking to key prospects with a regular flow of files.

New survey data reveals just how compelling that rate difference is—it's about 50 percent!

On average, senior partners at the mega firms, those with 400+ lawyers, charge clients 34 percent more per hour than senior partners at mid-size law firms, those with 150-399 lawyers. It jumps to an eye-popping 63 percent more than senior partners at smaller firm with less than 150 lawyers, according to a new study from BTI Consulting.

The difference is significant at all levels of lawyer experience. Junior partners at the mega firms charge 30 percent more than junior partners at mid-size firms and 51 percent more than junior partners at smaller firms. Associates at mega firms charge 22 percent more than associates at mid-size firms, BTI revealed, and 46 percent more than smaller law firms. This disparity is confirmed by other surveys including ALM's Survey of Law Firm Economics.

In-house counsel, savvy executives and closely-held business owners know most of their legal work is not "bet-the-company" and that smaller firms can and should handle the bulk of their legal assignments. Use the price differential, citing this data, in tandem with presenting your analysis, experience, industry and legal issue specific, along with your accessibility and local knowledge when you are competing against Big Law.

Who could justify paying twice as much for the same legal services and insights you provide? ◆

Differentiating Characteristics
You Might Use to Create a Brand

We hear a great deal of empty talk about "branding" law firms. Many seem to think it's all about a catchy tagline or snazzy signature image. Hundreds of firms spend tens of thousands of dollars in search of one or the other every year.

At the heart of branding any professionals service (or product) are four absolutes— truth, differentiation, meaning and durability. Whatever your brand statement or proposition it must be true, it must have a compelling meaning to your clients and referrals sources, and it must differentiate you from most all of your competitors while being able to endure the test of time.

Writing for hingemarketing.com recently, Lee Frederickson listed 21 differentiators that work for professional services firms. This is one of the best compilations of such factors I have ever read. You should consider using one or more of these to "brand" your practice, as Fredrickson advocates.

Fredrickson, who holds a doctorate and was a tenured professor at Virginia Tech, is managing partner of hinge®, which does branding and marketing for various professional services organizations. His 21 differentiators for organizational and personal branding are:

1. Specialize in an industry.

This is perhaps the easiest and most successful differentiator for most firms. Clients value the specialist in their industry. But be careful. If you try to specialize in too many industries, you will lose credibility.

2. Specialize in serving a specific role within your client's organization.

This role-based specialization is also quite successful, especially if combined with an industry focus. If you head IT at a law firm, it's comforting to know that your service provider specializes in helping people just like you.

3. Specialize in offering a particular service.

This is also quite successful, especially if the service you specialize in is rare and hard to find. But beware, unique service offerings can quickly become mainstream. Witness Sarbanes-Oxley compliance or social media marketing as two recent examples.

4. Offer a truly unique technology or process.

By truly unique, we do not mean your process that starts with assessment and ends with monitoring results and making adjustments. We mean an approach that is a whole different way of approaching the problem that offers a unique benefit to the client.

5. Focus on understanding a particular target audience.

A key differentiator for some firms is their in-depth understanding of a particular audience. Your firm might specialize in marketing to Baby Boomer women. Your clients might be retirement planners, insurance companies or clothing retailers, for example.

6. Specialize in serving clients of a certain size.

This is a common differentiator, although some folks don't think of it as such. Perhaps you work exclusively with the largest companies in the world. Contrast that with a firm that focuses on solo practitioners. Either firm could have a competitive advantage over the firm that serves clients of all sizes.

7. All of your staff shares a specific characteristic or credential.

Everyone feels like they have a great team. So it's tough to make that stick as a differentiator. But what if all of your programmers hold PhDs in Computer Science? That is both provable and meaningful to a potential client. Or perhaps all your project managers are PMPs. Not as distinctive, but also provable and relevant.

8. Specialize in clients that share a common characteristic.

This differentiator is focused on a characteristic of your clients other than their industry or role. Let's say you provide accounting and tax services for expatriates. They might be from any country, in any industry or any corporate role, yet you will have a competitive advantage.

9. Focus on solving a specific business challenge.

Here, the spotlight is not on the client as much as on the nature of the business challenge they are facing. To work, it must be a challenge that is easily recognized and tough to solve without specialized skills and experience. Helping firms secure their first government contract is an example.

10. Have one or more individuals who are high visibility experts in their fields.

This is a time-tested strategy that works very well. Having the country's top expert in your specialty is a very powerful competitive advantage. Many firms have been built on this differentiator alone. Add multiple high visibility experts and you will have a compelling and very valuable brand.

11. Offer a unique business model.

Everyone in your profession bills by the hour, but you offer a fixed fee. Voilà, a perfect differentiator is born! A unique business model can be both meaningful and easy to prove. But be watchful. If it works well, you are likely to accumulate imitators.

12. Have a specific geographic focus.

This is a very traditional differentiator that is losing some of its punch as technology and common business practices are making geography less important. But take heart, it can still work in situations where local knowledge or face-to-face interaction are still seen as important by potential clients.

13. Offer access to a unique set of information not available elsewhere.

Sometimes, access to certain information can be very valuable to potential clients. Do you have benchmarking data that no one else possesses? Some firms have built very valuable practices around proprietary data not easily duplicated.

14. Offer a unique set of contacts or relationships not easily accessible.

While the previous differentiator focused on information, this one is focused on relationships. Public relations firms have long used relationships with reporters and editors as differentiators. What relationships can your firm bring to the table?

15. Do business with a distinctive level of service.

In most cases, offering good client service is simply the price of entry. Everyone does it, or claims to. So to become a differentiator, your level of service really has to truly stand out. Can it be done? Indeed, there are still some physicians who make house calls.

16. Distinguish yourself by the clients you have.

Having an impressive client list is a plus for many firms. But what if you take it further? Some firms differentiate themselves based on their client list. For example, if your firm serves the higher education market and your clients are Harvard, Yale and Stanford, you have a differentiator.

17. Focus on the size of your firm.

We are the largest...fill in the blank. Size sends a signal that you are doing something right in the minds of many potential clients. This combines nicely with a specialization to show both relevance (the specialty) as well as success (the largest). Find a niche and dominate it.

18. Emphasize your relationship with a parent firm or partner.

A close relationship with a parent firm can be a limiter (potential clients may feel like you cannot be objective about other technologies for example). But for other potential clients, it can be a big asset. Who knows the ins and outs of the technology better? This same differentiator might also be applied to situations where your firm is a value-added partner rather than a subsidiary.

19. Focus on a notable signature accomplishment.

Some firms can build a strong brand based on achieving a notable accomplishment. Firms that invented a technology or solved a highly visible problem for a very well-known client are good examples. This type of notoriety can be leveraged throughout an industry and over time.

20. Specialize in producing a unique or very valuable result.

Similar to number 9, where you focus on a notable business challenge, this differentiator focuses on a valuable result. The key difference is that you may need to overcome multiple business challenges to produce the valuable result. For example, you might specialize in turning average growth clients into high growth firms. This could involve solving a wide range of business challenges, rather than a single one.

21. Look or act differently than all of your competitors.

Most professional services firms tend to look and act a lot like their competitors. Why? Perhaps you have been in the industry for a long time. Or perhaps doing things very differently feels risky. We see this all the time. Well, a very different look and feel can be a powerful differentiator for this exact reason. Combine this with other differentiators and you have the makings of a robust competitive advantage.

If true, meaningful and enduring these factors can be your brand. Chances are many readers of this article will see differentiators above that they already embody, which intuitively they understand are the basis of their success. Your next challenge becomes conveying these concisely and relentlessly over time in person, online, in all media reaching your organization, client and referral bases. ◆

Get Clients to Rate You on Martindale

We urge our clients have full listings on Martindale-Hubbell (MH) and consistently find when they do that website analytics reveal www.martindale.com and www.lawyers.com, MH's two online properties, are the single largest third-party sources of referral traffic to the law firm's website.

Numerous studies support that business owners and in-house counsel rely on MH and its ratings as much or more than any other directory or ratings when vetting new counsel or confirming a word-of-mouth referral before contacting a lawyer.

Getting an AV rating from MH is requisite, as most lawyers know. However, many lawyers have not taken the added and important step of obtaining a "Client Rating" on MH. This is a relatively new feature. It can only help to have such ratings—and you should ask satisfied clients if they'd take a few minutes to rate you on Martindale. Our experience is they're flattered you ask and happy to rate you.

Make it easy on the client. Go to your bio page on MH and copy the link to it out of your browser. Include that link in an email you send to your top clients. In your email ask them to go to your bio on MH. There they should look to the right where they can click on "Submit a review".

Should You Buy an Ad
in That Special Section or Publication?

Most often the answer is: No, no, no, one thousand times no.

We get calls from clients every week asking if they should advertise in a special advertising section of a national bar magazine, their daily paper, a weekly business journal or lifestyle magazine, because the firm or one of its lawyers have been given an award or designation by the publication. The ad, they were told by a friendly sales representative, will extend the value of the award or recognition. Also, to make it easy on you, the publication will write the ad and do the layout for free!

The awards often are economic contrivances designed by publications. They commonly appeal to lawyer's egos.

The exceptions are more than we can list here. Generally speaking, they are for awards based on an objective survey or by an independent panel of experts in an open competition, and only if recognizing truly meaningful professional standards or business accomplishments important to a broad section of your target market. Special sections publishing your selection to Best Lawyers®, for example, can make the grade. However, make sure the section is not just an insert designated a "Special Advertising Section," meaning by Rules of the American Society of Magazine Editors(ASME) designed to protect editorial integrity they are not noted on the publication's cover or in its table of contents.

If you have an annual ad program or special campaign you are already executing pursuant to an established plan and budget, keep to that schedule. Don't dilute that effort with unscheduled, opportunistic ads like these. If you don't have an ad campaign or program, the answer is obvious—you shouldn't be advertising at all. ◆

Should Your Firm Buy Advertising in a Local Economic Development Guide or Trade Magazine?

Absent having a robust social media program, solid presence in national bar and influential local trade groups, membership in a vibrant law firm network, holding the key peer-review ratings, a law firm will find itself with little choice but to consider comparably cost-inefficient marketing tactics, particularly trade directory and specialty magazine advertising.

We were reminded of this recently when a client was asked to buy advertising in a magazine created by their local economic development group to be given to companies considering relocating or expanding into their hometown.

For the law firm, the main question is how many people who might get these magazines might also be charged with or heavily influence the selection of a law firm that would then represent a company relocating to or expanding into your region. We think that number of people would be quite small. That means these magazines are not reaching your target audience and that most who are seeing the publication likely are not buyers of your services or major influencers in the choice of a law firm.

Even if the reach of these publications is greater than most imagine, the data available to us (from surveys by Cone, BTI Consulting and American Lawyer Media, among others) is consistent in showing such ads will be of little or no effect. The surveys clearly indicate that companies relocating or expanding into new jurisdictions where they do not currently have existing counsel will search for new lawyers by first asking their existing outside counsel for personal recommendations in the new market. After receiving names of lawyers or firms, most all of the c-level execs or in-house counsel of the relocating or expanding company then will go online. There they will confirm the capabilities of those lawyers and firms through Martindale and other peer-review directories and ratings. This is why we put such an emphasis on these directories and ratings in a law firm's marketing plan.

It is excellent positioning for your lawyers to be involved in regional economic development groups. If you can learn about a company considering a move into your market you can then see who in your law firm network or otherwise connected to one of your lawyers (think LinkedIn Connections) can get you that critical personal recommendation. This is also why it's important, if possible, to have your lawyers nominated to and active in national bar groups or colleges such as the American College of Real Estate Lawyers.

In the end, the legal business remains one based on personal recommendations backed up by a confirming comprehensive online presence. ◆

Are Ads Congratulating Clients an Opportunity or Arm-Twisting?

Should you buy an ad in a publication that is honoring your client when they are given your firm's name as being a key vendor?

There are two views here of this decades-old media practice, commonly seen in the construction community but being adopted elsewhere, and an ethics issue.

The first view is that the publication creates a list or honor that means little. The publisher then writes a puff profile of the "winning" company, in a special report no one really reads or relies upon. In the process, they identify suppliers and then put the arm on the suppliers to buy a congratulatory ad, putting the suppliers in a position of looking unsupportive of customers/clients if they do not advertise. This amounts to arm-twisting or "soft extortion" many suppliers and several law firms have told us over the years.

The other view is this allows the suppliers or law firm to explain or show they are an important element of a prominent, industry-leading client's success. This demonstrates to others in the industry who read the article that they should use or recommend the supplier or law firm.

Our experience and all of the data we have seen do not indicate such ads are an effective way to create referrals or retention. Frankly, your clients don't care if you buy an ad or not.

Question: can a law firm say or suggest it represents a company absent permission from the client; meaning is there an ethics issue here? Yes, your client gave the name of the firm to the publication, but the privilege rests with the client not the firm or publication and is not waived as a result, as we understand the rule. What can your ad ethically say, congratulations only? that you do defense work? that you do anything specifically? Did the clients know you would disclose the nature of your work?

The best course often lies somewhere in between the two views. You have to evaluate the client, the billings, the industry, the publication, the confidentiality and your budget, particularly if this sets the firm up for other unscheduled (often pricey) ads.

We tend to think firms should avoid these "opportunities." If you are an integral part of the client's team and success, the ad makes no difference in the relationship. Few of these articles are well read, so the ad's effect is commonly scanty beyond the client's reaction to it. Certainly recognizing the article was published; a personal note to key contacts in the firm, by the firm or lawyer makes sense. So does a case study on the firm's website. ◆

How Long Does It Take
for Marketing Efforts to Generate Revenue?

How long does it take for more formalized marketing efforts, individual or firm-wide, to generate revenue? It's a common and important question to get answered as you make the investment in updating or finally formalize marketing plans and initiatives.

With the possible exception of plaintiff cases, or specialty assignments caused by a statutory deadline, firms should not expect any results for 18-24 months from their newly written marketing plans or marketing initiatives. The reason: the truly desirable clients are already in working relationships with a lawyer or firm. I choose the word relationship on purpose here. There's trust in place.

Campaigns must convince prospects there's value in trying a different lawyer. The problem: most prospects likely will send the next matter they contemplate sending you, after being properly affected by your campaign, to their existing lawyer anyway. It's easier for them to do this; it involves again using a known quantity. It is familiar behavior, the latter perhaps the greatest (certainly not always the best) driver of business decisions.

It isn't until the next matter—the second matter the prospect contemplates sending you so your campaign has to be ongoing and running during the entire timeframe I am describing here—that you get the prospect to finally send you a new matter they previously would have sent to their existing firm.

The sales process, that being awareness/name recognition, then comprehension by a prospect that you can fulfill a need, then consideration when a matter arises and then, finally, retention for a case that could be sent to the existing lawyer takes time. In our experience that's like 18-24 months. Sooner results than that are fortunate, but not the norm. You have to create trust, and then be the chosen substitute in an existing relationship before you see any billable time result from your campaign(s).

Chapter 9:
Seminars and Open Houses

— ◆ —

How to Answer "What Do You Do for a Living?"

I recently learned a better way to remember and construct the answer to the most important and most common marketing question lawyers are asked.

The question is "What do you do?"

The answer: "I + (action word) + (target market) + (problem solved or benefit provided)."

Many call this answer your elevator speech. It's critical to practice it and have it at the ready. You've got to be able give your answer easily and without a hint of self-consciousness.

It's difficult to keep sufficient, simple and sincere. And you probably need to have more than one answer. The one you give will depend who asks you the question.

I recommend you practice it in the mirror or with your spouse or significant other. ◆

Nametags at Events Are Not Optional
and Keep Them Simple

I walked into a firm open house recently, after dutifully making a reservation as requested, and there was no check-in table or nametags for guests.

The firm's lawyers and staff were wearing nametags. Not one guest was given one, even when they asked if one was available. The hosts said the firm had decided it would be fun to make the guests "...work to find out who was there" and besides "...the event is about meeting us anyway."

The firm's guests had a different opinion.

They were frustrated and several mentioned how difficult the lack of nametags made conversation. Several lawyers from the host firm's other offices in the region didn't bother to wear nametags, and that just added further to the confusion.

We all forget names. It occurs even more often when you unexpectedly see someone out of normal context or dressed formally at an event. This can cause embarrassment. Why set your guests up for such stress?

In his article, the "Seven Deadly Sins of Ineffective Nametags," Scott Ginsberg, author of *The Power of Approachability*, says "Your nametag is your best friend. It is a lifesaver in meetings, trade shows and events to start conversations when you meet groups of new people. It also identifies you as well as your company in the minds of others. As a result, you will become more approachable so you can connect and communicate with anybody."

Nametags, Ginsberg adeptly explains, "...invite people to 'step onto your front porch,' and cross the chasm between a stranger and a friend or a prospect and a customer."

Common mistakes to avoid when doing nametags:

- Make the type big enough so it can be read from 8 to 10 feet away. If you are in one conversation and a face seems familiar across the room or if you are walking up to someone you want to be able to see that person's name so you can be ready to talk with him or her. According to a nametag survey done by David Alder of Biz Bash,

50 percent of a group of meeting planners claimed that "illegible font size of nametags was a major problem."

- Have you ever seen a billboard on a major highway with a solid border around the edges? Same rule applies to nametags, no borders.
- Another billboard rule: three elements only. The person's name is one, firm/company name is two and title/position or city can be third. No more.
- Sticking with the well-known billboard rules, the most effective background color for nametags is white. The human eye reads white (so-called reverse) type on a solid color background color half as fast.

A frustrating nametag problem that people face is "the nametag turn-around." No name. No logo. No company. You see just the blank back of the badge. "While lanyard or necklace style nametags reduce clothing damage, no doubt these will get accidentally turned around and tangled at some point!" Ginsberg says. Use sticky tags.

Wear nametags on the right where they are easily visible in the line of sight that correlates to a handshake. Wear it just below your shoulder line. Lower than that and your arms get in the way and it is hard to see if you are sitting. ◆

Tips for More Effective Seminars and Speeches

Our National Marketing Effectiveness Survey has long indicated that seminars and speeches are one of the most effective way to develop files for a defense or business practice and that they also create cases for contingent fee lawyers.

Here are three tips to improve your next seminar or speech:

1. If possible, make it qualify for continuing professional education credit. Nurses, human resource managers, therapists, physicians, CPAs, Realtors, adjustors, insurance agents, architects, engineers and many others need ongoing CE credits to maintain licenses or credentials. Think about who might attend your presentation and get it approved for as many in your potential audience as possible.

2. Keep the audience small, fewer than 20. Harvard University studied communication effectiveness and found that speakers made many more and far better connections to audiences of this size than to an auditorium full of folks. If you wind up in front of a bigger group, make sure you get down off the stage and into the crowd afterward, if not during, your talk.

3. The most effective advertising technique is a demonstration. That's why they show you the Kitchen Magician as "it slices and dices" on TV. Build a demonstration of what you do into your presentation (case studies with props, if possible).

4. Always negotiate obtaining a copy of the attendance list. If the sponsoring organization won't give it to you, have people who want more information email or text you—ask them to do it at the beginning and end of your talk.

Chapter 10:
Lawyer Ratings and Biographies

— ◆ —

Find, Claim and Cleanse Your Online Directory Listings

Most all state and local bar associations, and many notable national organizations, have abandoned their printed membership directories.

As a result every law firm marketing plan should have as a tactic to regularly find, claim and cleanse every online listing and profile related to its lawyers and the firm.

It's with good reason that printed memberships directories have moved online all of the information that was once in a book lawyers and professional staff routinely consulted and kept on their desks. This is because nearly all of this information can be obtained through direct inquiries via Internet search. And once online, it can be updated in real time.

These new online directories will be used, but many of the associations have few statistics to provide regarding traffic on their overall sites and specifically to these directories. Eventually they will share what traffic statistics they have so firms can evaluate the overall value of their memberships. Selling advertising within or adjacent to online directories is becoming an obvious revenue opportunity as well. Traffic statistics, just like circulation and viewership studies used by traditional broadcast media, will be generated to allow comparisons and spur these advertising sales. (We were taken aback in mid-2011 when we learned from the publisher no such statistics were available or contemplated concerning traffic to Best's Recommended Insurance Attorneys.)

While we wait for this transition and information, it's important to recognize the value of the inbound link to your website from a directory on a well-known, long-standing, credible, highly-trafficked website is not to be ignored. That kind of link from a major association or organization website helps your search engine optimization results. So you should make sure your firm and lawyers are correctly listed and links appear in these directories. ◆

Common Lawyer Bio Mistakes

We commonly see two mistakes in lawyer bios on firm websites, one related to ease of contact and the other regarding creating immediate credibility for a lawyer.

These are important to address because the most often visited pages on your site in sum, even more than total opens of your Home page, are lawyer bio pages. Also, the most common reasons visitors visit bios is to contact a lawyer to whom they have been referred or to vet just prior to initial contact. So, a best practice is to make contact via your bio page as easy as possible for a visitor and hit hard and fast regarding standing in the bar.

To ensure maximum chance of being contacted it's best to have either the lawyer's actual email address as a link (yourname@yourfirm.com) or a link (saying 'email your name', in addition to having the ability to download a vcard). Put this right at the top. Some firms force visitors to open a downloadable vcard. The problem: that means visitors have to click twice more to get to an open email form addressed to you—and several studies show the more often a visitor has to click to complete a transaction, the less likely they are to complete the process.

Visitors looking at your bio make up their mind about your credibility, about your standing in the bar and experience, in seconds. They were told you were right for the job by someone else and you need to confirm that ASAP. That means badges for Best Lawyers®, Super Lawyers®, and AV® Ratings need to be above the scroll, not down at the bottom of a bio page where they will not be seen by a visitor until that visitor (hopefully) spends time reading through your bona-fides.

These branded peer-review based images, plus a U.S. News Best Law Firm® badge are like pictures and worth 1,000 words each. In less than a second you know the lawyer whose bio you are about to read is top-drawer. We think you should move these up on everyone's bio so they are seen immediately every time a bio gets opened, including on mobile versions of your lawyer bios, if possible.

Yes, designers will say these icons clutter up the graphic beauty of what they are trying to do with your site. And, they probably are correct. After all, the badges were not designed with your website's design or color palette in mind. However, with apologies to all of the fine website designers we know, function over form wins out here.

Thoughts on the Proliferation and Value of Lawyer Ratings

Why has *Chambers USA* so quickly established widespread credibility? Super Lawyers and Martindale have programs in place to build their brands. The latter is even doing TV advertising to enhance the value and reach of their ratings and directories. Best Lawyers® also discretely markets its brand. Chambers seems to do it less aggressively than everyone else right now but seems equally successful.

I think one answer lies in the research on purchase habits of affluent and educated American consumers. That research reveals that when faced with a selection with which they associate a high degree of risk, such as hiring a CPA, lawyer, financial advisor, banker or selecting a doctor or dentist, affluent and educated buyers most always seek personal recommendations. (The author of the bestsellers *The Millionaire Mind* and *The Millionaire Next Door* published this research in another book on networking with the affluent and their advisors.)

Comparatively, the Chambers' interview process is closest of all to a personal recommendation. Martindale quickly sensed this and added client and lawyer reviews to its sites.

The proliferation of directories and lists like Chambers has not been without controversy. Many firms and lawyers have openly resisted them and pronounced participation as burdensome. Most all have eventually relented and participated on some level and in more than one list. Taken together, several lists can give even the most sophisticated buyer of legal services valuable information that may differentiate providers. That said, listings and ratings like this are no substitute for a robust online presence and detailed biography on your firm's website—think Google.

Our major concern, and that of many lawyers and firms we write marketing plans for across the country, is what we call "list fatigue." How many times each year can you ask the same lawyers in other firms and the same clients of yours to accept interviews about you and your firm or to fill out surveys on your behalf? Chambers limits the number of times it contacts references.

The lists make the practice of law more transparent and that's good for everyone who hires lawyers or makes referrals.

The overall demand for legal services far exceeds the service capacity of all of the top lawyers on any single list or in any single directory. Therein lies the case for the participation in and value of the other lists. Location, area of practice, size of firm and nature of client also creates good reasons to appear on particular lists, and not on others.

Finally, recent surveys indicated in-house lawyers and executives use these lists and directories regularly to vet counsel. Failing to be on the most popular—Martindale-Hubbell, Super Lawyers, Best Lawyers, and Chambers—"hinders" or makes retention "unlikely." ◆

Short Guide to Key Lawyer Directories and Rankings

Generally speaking, we advise firms maximize profiles and rankings on the platforms listed here. That's because independent surveys, our own surveys, our interviews with in-house counsel, c-level executives and business owners indicate these are commonly relied upon by prospective clients and referring counsel. Of course, how much effort and which directories and rankings you focus more time and money on depend on the nature of your firm's practice and the goals set forth in your law firm marketing plan.

SUPER LAWYERS

Where To Find It: Its list is often published in a local lifestyle magazine, as its own publication mailed to all lawyers in your state and online at www.superlawyers.com

What It Is: An annual online and print listing of the top 5 percent of the eligible attorney population for Super Lawyers, and 2.5 percent of the eligible attorney population for Rising Stars. Another 500 lawyers who score below Super Lawyers, but who are 40 years old or younger or have 10 fewer years of practice are designated Rising Stars.

Who Can Be Listed: Attorneys are eligible to be listed if they've been listed before or if another lawyer nominates them. By nominating someone else, attorneys also become part of the eligible pool.

How It Is Created: The research department reviews the candidate pool and scores them based on 12 categories, including verdicts, settlements, transactions, representative clients and honors and awards. Some of the categories are valued higher than others, but Super Lawyers won't reveal its formula for scoring.

Picks are sorted into practice areas and sent through a "blue ribbon review," a panel of candidates with the highest point totals in each practice area. Those panelists rank a list of candidates from their practice areas on a scale of one to ten.

A best practice is to make sure all of your firm's news releases and articles are submitted to their research department throughout the year. This helps build lawyer ratings.

Don't let the name fool you—people and other lawyers pay attention to this ranking. And if anyone tells you this is "pay to play" ranking, well, they're just flat wrong.

MARTINDALE-HUBBELL

Where To Find It: www.martindale.com and www.lawyers.com

What It Is: An ongoing print and online directory listing of attorneys by practice area. Also lists firms and solicits client ratings. Client ratings are an oft-controversial subject in many firms and beyond the scope of this article. Both subscribers and nonsubscribers to LexisNexis Martindale-Hubbell can get reviews, but a fee is charged to display lawyer ratings on a website and in marketing materials. This is the home of "AV", the longest-standing arguably most credible rating in the business.

Who Can Be Listed: Attorneys are eligible after three years of bar admission. They only need provide their practice area and bar admission year. To request a review, attorneys must also submit at least 18 peer references from lawyers listed in the directory which are outside their firm.

How It Is Created: Reviews are given by both request and random selection of attorneys according to their geographic location and practice area. All reviews are anonymous. Attorneys are rated via an online survey on a scale of 1 to 5 (with 5 being the highest) in five areas: legal knowledge, analytical capabilities, judgment, communication and legal experience. Reviewers selected by Martindale-Hubbell are already listed.

Only attorneys with average scores of 4.5 to 5.0 obtain the AV Preeminent designation. Those with averages of 3.0 to 4.4 used to earn the BV Distinguished rating and the rest receive a rating showing that the attorney at least meets a "very high criteria of general ethical standing." BV was eliminated in 2016.

NOTE: Getting an adequate response to establish or improve an existing rating has become more difficult in the past 24 months following Martindale's decision to make it ratings questionnaire more elaborate. This has become of source of some frustration to lawyers and in the marketing community of late.

BEST LAWYERS

When It Appears: September annually

Where To Find It: Several years ago they partnered with US News & World Report to create Best Law Firms rankings by practice area (http://bestlaw-firms.usnews.com/) in addition to the list of The Best Lawyers in America (http://www.bestlawyers.com/) which is now called simply Best Lawyers.

What It Is: Although Best Lawyers doesn't set quotas on the number of attorneys per jurisdiction, they list an average of 3.5 percent of the total attorneys in the U.S. Like Super Lawyers, Best Lawyers is based on peer reviews. (Firm rankings are handled through client interviews.)

Who Can Be Listed: Attorneys on the previous year's list are automatically entered and are also asked to include names of peers who were not yet nominated. Marketing departments can also submit nominations, selectively. Up to three names can be submitted on the form and nominees not included in the list remain on the ballot for the next two editions.

How It Is Created: Attorneys on the previous year's list get to vote on attorneys from their respective practice areas and regions. More than 30,000 attorneys evaluate nominees on a scale of 1 to 5 based on the question, "If you could not handle a case yourself, to whom would you refer it?" with 5 being the highest.

Evaluations are compiled, averaged and checked against state bar association sanction lists and ethics committees. The filtering process is different for each geographic region. Required score averages vary for each region and in the case of "close calls," Best Lawyers editors will also take into consideration comments made by other attorneys.

Lawyers we know and represent who have been named to this list report it changes how other lawyers view them and improves the quality and scope of their case flow.

AVVO

Where To Find It: www.avvo.com

What It Is: An online ranking of attorneys in every state. AVVO's rating system is based on public information and are not influenced by advertising on the service, as some believe. For example, an associate several years into a practice who makes an effort can have a higher AVVO rating than a senior partner at a large law firm who does not.

How It Is Created: You have an AVVO profile. AVVO created it using public information from the state bar licensing database and other legal credentialing organizations.

Your AVVO rating depends on the amount of information provided by third parties and by you. It is displayed on a scale of a 1.0–"Extreme Caution" to 10.0–"Superb". Ratings are given using a mathematical model derived from an attorney's background including practice areas, ethics, client reviews and past experience.

AVVO ratings cannot be changed or deleted, but scores may be increased when attorneys provide more information about themselves. Clients and fellow attorneys can also give their own separate endorsements that show up alongside and boost a lawyer's overall AVVO rating.

Those lawyers about whom there is little public information, commonly in-house counsel, receive a non-numerical "No Concern" rating. But those with ethics violations or other disciplinary actions will receive a non-numerical "Attention" rating.

Who Is Listed: Creating an improved profile with AVVO—short for "avvocato or avvocatessa," the Italian words for lawyer—can be done at no cost. All that's required to begin enhancing an existing profile is some basic confirming information.

Don't ignore your AVVO rating. It probably shows up on page one of Google search results when your name and city are typed into a browser search bar.

CHAMBERS USA

Where to Find It: www.chambersandpartners.com

What It Is: An annual print and online listing of about 1 percent of total attorneys in your state. Unlike Best Lawyers or Super Lawyers, client, not peer, interviews and reviews drive Chambers.

Who Can Be Listed: Firms, not individual attorneys, drive the process, by submitting lengthy nominations including information about the firm's recent laterals, departures and highlights of the year's biggest cases. A spreadsheet of up to 15 references should also be included.

How It Is Created: After submissions are received, the Chambers USA research team conducts telephone interviews with clients and other references. Some factors taken into consideration: volume, marketplace commentary, info gleaned from interviews and the complexity and size of last year's work.

The research team looks at practice area-specific factors such as industry-significant cases, expansion in team size or the development of new areas of specialty. Chambers USA annually interviews more than 16,000 clients and 10,000 private-practice attorneys.

After the interviews, selections get whittled down to a select few attorneys separated by practice area, which usually amounts to about 1 percent of total attorneys per state. The top attorneys are ranked in "bands" from 1 to 6, with 1 being the highest.

These are top lists from all of the data we've seen as of this writing. ◆

Attention All AV Lawyers – You Can Lose Your Rating

You may not remember that you (and a number of your partners) were among tens of thousands of attorneys who were assigned an AV-5.0 rating in 2010 when Martindale-Hubbell added a numerical component to its designations.

When Martindale announced that modification, they also said they would begin randomly re-rating all lawyers with AV designations at some future point. That time has come and all lawyers given an AV-5.0 in 2010 will be re-rated in the next few years.

I am writing this because numerous partners around the country have recently missed or ignored emails sent to them by Martindale announcing they were being re-rated. A couple of months later they have received a notice they had lost their AV or, due to a lack of response by those lawyers Martindale unilaterally decided to poll, now had no rating at all. To say these lawyers were upset was a profound understatement. It's happening to well-known competent partners who have been in practice at prominent firms for decades.

If you get a re-rating email, get your marketing people involved ASAP. They will work with you to assure proper polling occurs. You can and must submit to Martindale your own list of lawyers outside of your firm and, if possible, judges who know your work. These votes are essential if you are to keep your AV designation.

A full explanation of Martindale's new rating system is at:

http://www.martindale.com/Products_and_Services/Peer_Review_Ratings.aspx

Who's Who: All Are Lame, a Shame and a Waste of Time and Money

Every month attorneys we represent are solicited to buy or confirm listings in various editions of "Who's Who."

Don't be tempted. Save your marketing dollars. And delete any listing from your website biography or resume, and do it immediately.

What was once a respected research tool more than a decade ago has joined the gallery of famous lost trademarks. Today, most anyone can get into "Who's Who," and there are dozens of versions of the once-thick reference books you saw in the library. Few find their way onto library research shelves any longer. Many are seldom referenced and are nothing but obscure online lists.

An article in Forbes more than a decade ago revealed just who is in "Who's Who," a pipefitter, driver's education instructor, even imposters. The review and approval process has become scanty. It's funny to read:

http://www.forbes.com/fyi/1999/0308/063.html.

How did this happen?

The title "Who's Who" is now in the public domain. The result is that various authors and publishers have printed thousands of "Who's Who" compilations of varying scope and quality. Most of these are obvious vanity publications, where the inclusion criterion is a professional's willingness to buy the book and the business model consists of selling books directly to those who are listed.

So, next time you are asked to apply for a "Who's Who" listing remember, so was everyone else.

Chapter 11:
Working With In-house Counsel

---◆---

In-house Counsel:
"Lawyer, Not Firm Size, Is What Matters"

An in-house counsel has finally said publicly, in a prepared statement appearing in national media, what so many of us who are marketing boutique and small firms have long known—that it's not always best to hire a big firm when faced with big exposure.

Quoted in the *National Law Journal*, an in-house counsel for Sherwin-Williams says he's staying with his lawyer who has formed a boutique and is leaving the 11-office international law firm Milbank Tweed.

"It's all about Greg and his abilities, not the fancy firm and its high prices. In our environmental cases, we need people like Greg who put us first and get us the best results. Often, big firms just seem to get in the way of this kind of extremely valuable relationship."

The Milbank litigation partner said he felt "unbearable tension" between big law firm profits and the needs of clients.

"When companies have been cutting so many employees and budgets, which include legal budgets, I have seen—not just at Milbank, but across the industry—reluctance to adapt to what should be a new model of representing the legal interests of businesses.

"I want to, in this model, connect more closely with my clients and avoid the unbearable tension at times between a big firm profit model and the needs of businesses that are suffering through difficult economic times, whose legal affairs must be managed effectively and efficiently."

The boutique's operating formula is going to include a willingness to get paid on contingency or partial contingency, reduced billing rates, or performance-based bonuses. Those are tactics we often include when writing marketing plans for law firms competing with national firms. ◆

In-house Counsel's Latest Thoughts on Hiring Smaller Firms

I was talking recently with an in-house lawyer who controls a national litigation docket about the process of finding cost-effective representation in local and regional firms versus defaulting to the seeming safety and ease of finding lawyers in higher-rate national shops. I mentioned the vetting attendant to membership in the better national networks of independent firms and ability to find great lawyers there at lower rates. He went that route and wrote me back:

"Thanks again for the referral. Almost a case study—recommendation from someone you trust on a small matter, they do a good job, don't gouge, earn trust, evolves into bigger matters. It's funny because I was discussing this exact issue with our CLO and some of our senior guys the other day. CLO is from (a 50 lawyer Midwest firm), other guys are from (big firms in NYC), and was interesting to hear the biases. I think that once we get over the rate and specialty discussions, it really comes down to marketing yourself as doing something very well, and selling that. It seems more difficult for the smaller firms to be the jack of all trades that a 1,000 or 2,000 attorney international firm can be, but if they are the best at what they do, and have adequate resources, there really isn't a reason that they can't win the bet-the-company type of litigation. Also, we've recently had some smaller firms oversell. Difficult balance, but being shortsighted to win business that you can't successfully manage has caused some issues for firms that could definitely have made it up down the road. Just my initial thoughts and some recent experience as I try to manage within my budget, which is seeming to require changes from the previously accepted norms."

Lots of lessons in there as you market to corporate legal departments.

My firm's National Marketing Effectiveness Survey confirms membership in a law firm network is a best practice and we include seeking and maintaining membership in every law firm marketing plan we write. ◆

Interview: How One In-house Counsel and a National Defense Coordinator Find a New Law Firm

I recently talked with a general counsel and her outside national co-ordinating counsel for a national docket of litigation about how they hire and drop local firms. They assign 5,000 cases every year of which about 100 go to trial.

When searching for a new firm they create an initial list by asking other lawyers, both in-house and in private practice around the country, for references. They want the name of a lawyer, the person who will be their lead counsel, not a firm name. Once they have those names they cut the list down to four to six lawyers by selecting only lawyers at firms where a number of litigation partners are members of groups in which membership is vetted, such as IADC rather than not, such as DRI. (They said they use firm websites to discover this information.)

An evaluation of rates, industry experience, availability, conflicts and interviews come next. Their point to me was absent the personal references and vetted memberships, lawyers don't get considered. (This is consistent with our National Marketing Effectiveness Survey that shows trade group membership is one of the most effective marketing tactics a lawyer can employ.)

Asked why they most commonly drop a firm, they said failure to follow billing guidelines and over aggressive billing of associates and paralegals.

Asked if absence from key directories and having peer review ratings made any difference they agreed it could, other things mentioned here being equal. ◆

Effectively Market to In-house Counsel Through Your Pro Bono Work

Intel's innovative approach to pro bono work for its in-house lawyers, given a little twist, presents every firm with a way to accomplish its community service goals while concomitantly developing or maintaining relationships with in-house counsel.

Several years ago, the computer chip maker successfully used a request for proposal to find law firms to partner with in-house attorneys at its Silicon Valley headquarters on pro bono projects. The response was so gratifying that Intel later announced it would expand the program to other locations. Attorneys from Nixon Peabody and Baker & McKenzie were reportedly working with Intel lawyers on projects for two San Francisco-based public interest groups, Legal Services for Entrepreneurs and Legal Services for Children. Baker & McKenzie had worked with Intel before but not Nixon Peabody.

The opportunity for private firms here is not to wait for an in-house legal department or counsel whom they would like to get to know better to copy Intel's idea. Instead, private firms should contact in-house counsel about selecting and then working together on a project of mutual interest. The in-house lawyers don't have to be your clients.

The offer will fill a need. A survey of Intel's domestic legal staff had revealed many of the company's lawyers had once done and enjoyed pro bono projects when employed by outside law firms. The interviews of in-house lawyers we have conducted confirm Intel's lawyers are not alone. Pro bono opportunities are not presented to or actively sought by most large corporate legal departments or in smaller corporate counsel offices. The in-house lawyers we interviewed also said that working together on pro bono cases would build or further trust and confidence with an outside lawyer, and probably turn into paying work in the future.

"This really is a model," Esther Lardent, president of the Pro Bono Institute, told the *National Law Journal*.

Litigation isn't the only type of work to consider. Non-profits supporting low-income communities need to help people with, among other things, real estate transactions, employment, business, school and elder law.

———— ◆ ————

Chapter 12:
Marketing by Younger Lawyers

—◆—

How Younger Lawyers Can Help Your Firm's Marketing

A just-released survey on personnel trends by one of the legal industry's largest consulting firms indicates that a lasting result of the Great Recession is going to be that younger lawyers will be expected to help firms develop business earlier in their careers than in the past.

Abraham Reich, co-chair of 475-lawyer national firm Fox Rothschild, summed it up in telling www.law.com, "When I first started out as a lawyer, the mantra was, 'Don't worry about generating business, we have more than you can handle so just service our existing clients.' But now, young lawyers are being told that having a role in generating business should be on their radar screens."

Reich and the managing partners we work with writing law firm marketing plans for corporate, business and defense firms of all sizes indicate that their firms are keenly interested in retaining associates who can help a firm's marketing efforts. That's because associates commonly are more profitable than non-equity partners, the latter tending to bill fewer hours and generate lower profits, according to various surveys.

Here are a couple of things associates can consider right now to build relationships that may eventually lead to business or which will immediately lend important support to their firm's overall marketing efforts:

1. Not everyone can be an effective public rainmaker, or wants to be one. Some lawyers are great at meetings, clubs, and receptions, shaking hands and making conversation. Not everyone has to shake hands in order to effectively participate in rainmaking. Help your firm's public rainmakers, those equity partners deciding which associates they see having long-term value to their firm, by researching and writing articles, presentations and speeches and generating Web content. We discuss this kind of critical "behind the scenes" work in greater detail on our *Legal Marketing in Brief* blog at www.themarketinggurus.com in a post headlined "Value of Nontraditional Marketing Roles." It's also appears earlier in this book.

2. If you'd rather work toward a more public marketing role, ask yourself what file you have worked on that most interested you. In what industry was that client? Discover the key trade organization for that industry. Join it so you can become industry conversant. Survey after survey shows that executives and in-house lawyers prefer to hire outside counsel who know their industry, not just the legal issues. They don't want to pay to educate you in industry jargon and the business trends with which they are dealing. Don't know which trade organization makes the most sense? Ask your client what trade group they're a member of and find most important to their success—that's probably the one you'd want to look at joining.

As Reich put it, "It's not going to be back to business as usual in the legal profession." as we work our way past the Great Recession. ◆

Let Your Younger Attorneys Participate
in the Firm's Marketing

(This article was written by Amber Vincent, my partner and a Millenial herself.)

I have conducted numerous marketing surveys of lawyers within a firm and the same message rings true in each associate and young partner survey—"I WANT TO PARTICIPATE!"

Many of the firms that we have helped over the years come to us with the same issue, "Our young attorneys don't market, they don't write articles and they don't get out and shake hands with potential clients."

While this statement may seem to be true, it is not a reflection of a young attorney's ability to network in person. Instead it is the reality that technology has taken networking to a different platform.

The young lawyer generation was born and raised with computers, Internet, Google, Facebook, LinkedIn, blogs, email and text messaging all in their iPhones, iPads and Droids.

We don't know how to do anything different. We don't know how to type on a typewriter. Many of us have never used one. We don't know how to burn the rubber on the soles of our shoes while running from networking event to networking event.

We do, however, know how to set-up a blog, shoot website video, write blog content, design PowerPoint presentations, Google anything in a matter of seconds and many of us learned to write HTML code in our high school website design class. We are fluent in the world's new technology.

The foundation of a law firm has been built on the older generation's blood, sweat and tears. They have created the word-of-mouth referrals and personal relationships that actually make a successful law firm.

Younger partners and associates agree with, and appreciate, the older generation providing them with the amazing opportunity of practicing law at their firm. Many times, the next generation just wants the same opportunity to bring new life and energy into the firm through new marketing ideas and techniques.

Technology is a crucial, and often missing, part of a firm's marketing. Young lawyers understand that buyers, both consumers and in-house alike, credential and retain their lawyer through online vetting.

With all that being said, we do believe that the business of law is, and always will be, a relationship business. We hang out with classmates just as our mentors did. Technology does not excuse younger attorneys from making personal connections and creating relationships with individuals. Ideally, technology should be allowed and encouraged to create and simplify marketing opportunities.

If an associate can make their required billable hours while sitting in their office, and at the same time connect with and set up lunch with two law school alumni on LinkedIn, why not allow this type of networking?

The generation gap has caused significant disruptions in every size law firm for years. This can be addressed by encouraging the traditional model of personal networking, while embracing the ease that technology and innovation now provide lawyers of all ages.

Chapter 13:
Dealing with the Press

———— ◆ ————

Assume You're On the Record
When Talking to the Press or Bloggers

Many professionals do not understand the rules that govern giving information to the press or bloggers, the latter being what former professional journalists like me now call "citizen journalists."

If you have sensitive information you want to confidentially convey to a reporter, editor or blogger (the latter who generally have no formal training or interest in the rules of journalism), we recommend you get an experienced media relations professional to help you do it. If you don't have the funds or time to do that here is how the editor-in-chief of *The American Lawyer* explained "on the record" versus "on background" versus "off the record" conversations with journalists. Prior to being named editor-in-chief of *The American Lawyer*, he was a senior editor at *Newsweek*.

"When I talk to one of your lawyers, I assume everything's on the record. It's no good calling me two hours later to tell me that everything was 'off the record.' This happens all the time. If you establish up front that we're talking 'on background,' this means the reporter can use the material but not attribute it to you. If you're talking 'off the record' it means they can't use the material unless they discover it through another source. But the assumption is that, like in a courtroom, everything is on the record."

Personally, I find many citizen-journalists, writers and bloggers not formally affiliated with a formal news gathering organization and untrained in these rules. Dealing with them can prove problematic. Get professional help! Proceeding *pro se* is inadvisable. ◆

"Getting in the Newspaper"

National Public Radio once pointed out that Pres. Obama had not given an interview to *The Washington Post* in four years but had recently interviewed on Amazon for its Kindle Singles interview service. The next time one of your lawyers talks about the importance of "getting in the newspaper" keep that in mind. Perhaps remind that lawyer *The Post* was sold recently. The buyer: Jeff Bezos, Amazon's founder.

Legacy media is dying. The nightly gathering of American families around the TV at dinner to watch one of three network national news shows is gone, as is the ritualistic reading and discussion of events from the morning newspapers over coffee at breakfast. There is an official White House videographer; that's right videographer not photographer. The Pew Center reports that in July, *The Cleveland Plain Dealer* announced that it was cutting a third of its reporting, the (Portland) *Oregonian* announced in June that it was cutting 45 newsroom staff and the *Chicago Sun-Times* let its entire 28-person photo staff go in May.

Here's more on the Obama interviews, a transaction that a generation ago would have created a storm of ethical debate in the nation's journalism schools, many of which including my alma maters, have now been closed:

http://www.theblaze.com/stories/2013/08/01/166k-for-an-exclusive-obama
-interview-amazon-employee-campaign-donations-revealed/

❖

Get Maximum Media Coverage for You and Your Firm

Media coverage, including posts, comments and links with influential bloggers can create credibility for lawyers and firms, and result in file and case inquiries. Here's the outline of a mechanism that can help maximize traditional and online media coverage for you and your firm:

1. Create a list of publications and blogs, including any key trade publications of your clients and referral sources, which when they cover law/legal issues you want to ensure contact you for comment or contribution.

2. Obtain the advance editorial and special section calendars of each publication. Some will have calendars but some won't.

3. Have as a standing agenda item at your Marketing Committee meetings to review the editorial calendars and the upcoming special editions at each. Specifically discuss which you might participate in or to which you might contribute articles or expert comment. If you do contribute, keep your copyright.

4. In addition to addressing scheduled coverage, have as a standing agenda item at Marketing Committee to discuss trends, filings/rulings/decisions (whether you or your firm were involved or not) and about which you might alert writers of the influential publications or blogs.

5. Try to have an ongoing conversation with key editors and writers at the influential publications and blogs about what your firm sees happening. A couple of times annually will do. Most of the time this effort will not be to obtain coverage but be "background" to help them understand business transactions and trends and changes to the law. The message is something like: "Here are three things we see and about which you might want to be aware..." This would be done by lawyers over coffee, on the phone or even simply

by email. Make sure someone is listing the editors and writers and which lawyer talks with them. Yes, this is much easier said than done since the media bluntly and universally tells me lawyers historically only talk to them when it's to their immediate advantage. This process I've outlined can help you get past that. You have to become a resource to them. They understand you can't talk about clients and pending deals and cases. ◆

Maximizing Your Media Presence: What to Do After You Are Quoted or Place an Article

It's exciting and builds credibility to be quoted in the daily paper, on a prominent blog or to have an article appear in the local business journal or a trade association newsletter with your name on or in it.

To get maximum value from such media placements, however, you have to "merchandise the coverage." You can't assume all of your colleagues, clients and referral sources will read the paper that day, see that month's newsletter or have alerts or feeds to the blog.

If you write and place articles or are quoted as an expert some advance planning is in order. Make sure you retain or share copyright to any contributed work. After it appears, post it to your website and publish it on LinkedIn®. If the publisher will give you the right to make copies you should send them out attached to an email or with a cover note or letter attached saying "I thought you'd find my article from NAME OF PUBLICATION/BLOG discussing TOPIC." Many publications sell attractive reprints you can buy. Ask about them.

Distribute your article to colleagues, clients and referral sources. They need fresh reasons to justify their referral and working relationships with you—media coverage is one of the best ways to encourage referrals and retain existing clients. ◆

Getting Published Is a Great Achievement But Before You Start Writing Articles, Consider These Tips to Ensure Your Efforts Have Maximum Marketing Effect

To ensure your article-writing and guest blogging efforts are as valuable as possible, consider the following best practices we have learned from our clients in the defense, contingent fee and transactional bar nationwide:

- Before you publish, make sure the topic will have impact on the day-to-day activities of clients and referral sources. If it doesn't, if it's bar review-like, why would anyone who'd want to hire or refer you read it? Your topic is a chance to reveal your ability to think ahead and solve real-world problems, just as you would think ahead if you were the reader's counsel.

- Contact several clients and referral sources before you start writing. Explain where the article is to appear and what you plan to emphasize. Ask them what issues or angles might be added to the article. Contact not only people with whom you are in regular contact but those with whom you have allowed relationships to wither or with whom you'd like to establish a relationship. As one leading lawyer coach says, articles are "catalysts for conversations." Invite your colleagues to suggest people you might contact for input as well.

- After the article is published, obtain copies and send them to clients and key referral sources with a handwritten note or letter. Have your colleagues do the same. In the note or letter ask for feedback and for suggestions about other articles they'd like to see. If you're comfortable doing it, ask recipients for names of others who they may know who would be interested in receiving a copy of the article. This is a real BEST practice. Surveys show that top rainmakers are far more likely to ask for introductions to potential clients than colleagues who generate less business.

- Finally, consider social media. It would be rare for an article not to be suitable to publish on LinkedIn®.

Writing an article is an interactive process and incorporating these best practices into your writing efforts will ensure it leads to new business for you and your firm. ◆

When Is the Right Time to Notify the Media About Good News in Your Practice? It May Not Be as Often as You Think

Some of the most delicate media relations situations for legal marketers involve explaining that a transaction just completed, a ruling or verdict just won, an award just received or a donation just made, is not newsworthy, and that it is counterproductive to contact media or even post the information on the firm's website.

The second-most difficult thing to explain to attorneys is why the press or a blogger quoted someone that your attorney believes is less expert than he or she. This situation is exacerbated when your attorney has been contacted in the past and quoted in coverage on the same issue and by the same writer.

One of the best recognized media relations trainers for PR people addressed these issues in Tactics, the monthly news magazine of the Public Relations Society of America.

"See your press releases and story angles from the journalists' (or bloggers') point of view. Does this story benefit anyone but your company?" said Margo Mateas, president of the Public Relations Training Company. "Structure your pitch so it paints you in a positive light but also carries a message for other people."

To be blunt, "Stop being self-centered." she said.

Exceptions to this rule are certain niche publications, trade journals, alumni magazines, blogs and bar newsletters, all of which are devoted to covering people in an industry. Such publications are not generally circulated and promoted as are daily papers and weekly business journals and their sites. TV news programming also is mass circulated.

What the deal indicates, in terms of a business trend, or what influenced certain terms or its timing, is newsworthy. How a ruling or verdict may affect public policy or forces businesses or executives to modify operations is news. That's what you must discern and convey to a writer.

It is also important to understand that a steady stream of copy to bloggers, producers and editors will not increase the likelihood of coverage.

"The more you paper a newsroom or the more you pester a blogger, the more resistance and resentment you will encounter." Mateas said. "Reduce your media contact only to what is necessary. Pick your spots."

And, why did that reporter quote someone else, someone you think has only a fraction of your knowledge on the subject? Editors want their reporters to obtain more than one view of a situation. Further, over time, many attorneys become overly cautious in the quotes they give—and writers survive by providing punchy, provocative, pithy comments.

Despite changes in technology, the role of media, that being to inform and entertain, will not change.

Chapter 14:
Holiday Season Marketing—
Cards and Gifts

———— ◈ ————

Research Shows Gift and Card Giving Is a Requisite and
Shows How Much You Value the Client Relationship

If it's October and you have not thought about sending holiday cards and gifts to your key clients and referral sources, you are already falling behind in your holiday season marketing.

"Bah, humbug!" you say to this effort?

Well, consider some research I found about cards and gift giving. If you agree with it, and I think you will, then follow my best practices for both.

"Cards and gifts are a regular occurrence, even expected, for heads of state. They create and cement alliances, allegiances and partnerships," according to *The Psychology of Persuasion*.

But cards and gifts also are the "red-hot center of holiday hell," says the *Journal of Consumer Research*. Why?

Cards and gifts are a torturous endeavor because they create anxiety. The reason: senders are generally "highly motivated to elicit desired reactions from recipients." the *Journal* said.

The key is that whatever you do must "reflect the recipient's perceived value of relationship." the *Journal* concluded, adding that the proper gift must surprise the recipient and demonstrate familiarity with their tastes. For example, give a wine enthusiast a subscription to *Wine Spectator*, the leading vino ratings magazine.

If you're convinced now that gifts and cards are a good idea, here are some suggestions for proper distribution.

First, create a list of your top clients, balancing them in terms of fees paid, potential fees, referrals made and potential referrals they could make on your behalf. Also, list your existing and potential co-counsel and referring lawyers. Add in other professionals and advisors and you're off to an excellent start.

Send them all a holiday card. Under no circumstances should your card have just your firm's name at the bottom or lack a signature and personal note. Recipients will judge your card, and how you value your relationship, in direct proportion to the effort they think you put into sending it. Your first name in pen simply at the bottom doesn't do much good either and may hurt you. It shows you have no idea, when you were signing the card, who might get it, that you treat clients en masse, not individually, or you're too busy to take a moment to reflect. Is that the message you want to send, "I'm too busy to reflect fully on the situation?"

One year I received a card with signatures of attorneys preprinted on it. Unsigned cards are nothing but ads in the guise of holiday cards. How distant and disappointing it is to receive them.

Another I obtained had the lawyer's name signed with auto-pen software. That was an all-time low in my experience. It's how politicians send their self-serving direct mail to constituents. If you want your clients to think of you as they do a politician, I guess that will work. I can't imagine that's the response you want.

Does this mean you have to take time when it comes to holiday cards? You bet. I know lawyers who spend an entire day at it. And, every one that does is highly successful. It's worth every moment because a card or gift is far more than just a card or gift, as the research shows.

"Bah, humbug?" How about "Order now!" ◆

Law Firm Holidays Cards: Mistakes and Best Practices

I received three Thanksgiving cards from three different firms. One was a custom design that made an extremely positive impression, the other two were the SAME stock card.

In a prior article published by the ABA, I addressed best practices to ensure that holiday cards contribute to lawyer personal business development and explained where they fit into a law firm marketing plan. The cards I describe above bring up additional concerns I have not previously addressed.

First, you don't want to convey that you treat clients in a cookie-cutter fashion. You run the risk of this when buying a standardized card from a stock printer.

Second, skip the mass signing absent at least one signatory writing something personal to the recipient. One of the cards I received was signed by seven people, none of whom I recognize. It has the firm's name on it. I looked it up on the Internet and do not recognize the firm. Bad mailing list!

The good card? It had pictures of firm members as they worked on various pro bono and charity projects over the past year. On the back, it explained each event and the non-profit's mission. Classy. These people think about what they are doing, they prepare. Perfect messaging. I read the summaries, spent five minutes with the card and feel more positive about the firm than I did before.

Other holiday greeting card approaches that work year after year: one of our clients has holiday scenes painted by its lawyers, another shows art created by spouses or commissioned and then donated to a non-profit to be sold. These always get a great response. Pictures of your people also get consistently high marks—yes, high marks. Firms that invest in the holiday greeting card process get positive feedback.

In the end, our recommendation is to do a better (custom) card, preferably mailed, to a controlled (small) mailing list. Treating it as a mass mailing just does not get the job done, and may wind up being a negative. ◆

Getting Multiple Lawyers to Sign a Single Holiday Card

As you know, getting your attorneys to sign and include a personal note to the recipient of every holiday card (a best practice we recommend) is exceedingly difficult. Getting multiple signatures on cards sent to those who work regularly with more than one attorney in your firm, which we also urge, can prove even harder.

We have an answer that has been employed by several of our clients and confirmed as effective by other marketers, a Holiday Card Signing Party. Here are some points to consider when you do this.

1. Schedule a couple of specific times when attorneys can come in to sign. Most firms do it at lunch, say, between 11:30 and 1:30.

2. Decorate the room a little, just to make it somewhat festive.

3. Have some seasonal music playing. Otherwise, the room will be silent and somber and you don't want that!

4. Feed them. It's amazing how motivated some people are by adult beverages (afternoon events only, of course) and light snacks.

5. Prepare, prepare, prepare. Group the cards in advance by signer. In pencil, write the initials of each signer in the postage stamp area or on a sticky note. As the attorney signs, have him or her erase their initials.

Inevitably, you will have to route the cards around to pick up the stragglers, but mostly firms report their attorneys are cooperative and respectful of the effort and process. ◆

Discuss Who is Coming in Advance
to Maximize the Value of Your Holiday Party

To get maximum marketing value from an open house or holiday party—the most expensive business development efforts in which most law firms engage—hold an all-attorney meeting several days before to review which clients and referral sources will be attending.

At this meeting, have lawyers (quickly) explain the nature of their client's business operations, what they know of the client's business plan, the services that the firm provides the client and what additional services the firm might offer. A client you have defended in litigation for many years may have decided to expand regionally and need help with transactions or may be facing management succession issues and need tax and estate planning.

If the need for additional services is on the horizon, make it a priority to introduce a new lawyer at the event who can help the existing client. (Warning: make sure the new lawyer studies the client before the event. This will ensure the lawyer can demonstrate your firm's institutional knowledge of the client's industry, competition and operations.)

When you are done with this meeting, expect that a few prime cross-selling opportunities will have been identified. Most important, your lawyers will know the firm's clients better than ever and understand what they do and what the firm does for them. That knowledge will help everyone market the firm, not only at your open house or holiday party, but all year long.

Don't focus just on potential clients. Referral sources are part of this same equation. Discuss them at your pre-event meeting and make efforts to cross-sell them as well. ◆

Getting the Most Out of Your Holiday Party Conversation

Lawyers often tell us they are frustrated after conversations at events where they have spent considerable time and energy with existing and potential referral sources. The frustration expressed is even greater when the lawyers meet a prospective client. During the holiday social season these frustrations are often magnified.

The reason for the frustration is that lawyers understand they could be establishing or furthering a professional relationship from some of these conversations. However, they say they just cannot comfortably swing the topics discussed from the weather, children, sports or recent news events to mutual business interests.

Eventually, the lack of return on time invested becomes so discouraging that many lawyers quit attending functions or just assume no one wants to talk business there. They founder into that unfocused talk of sports, celebrities, bar gossip and vacation plans.

Here's a basic four-step process which, with just a bit of practice, will help you learn the important information you need. It will also allow you to tell your story when needed in conversation at cocktail parties, receptions and trade or community group meetings.

Remember we're not suggesting this is all you should say. We are saying keeping this process in mind will help lawyers get information they can use to build their referral base and allow them to convey meaningful facts about their firms and practices.

After initial introductions or greeting someone you know, wait until it feels comfortable and try to ask "Can you describe your ideal customer/client?"

After you have that answer, ask "Are there two or three things I might commonly hear that would indicate someone might be an ideal customer/client of yours?"

After hearing that answer, ask "Assume I hear someone say the things that would make them appear to be an ideal customer/client, what is the best way to introduce them to you?"

Of course, if the person you ask these questions doesn't ask you the same ones back, you should take charge and say "Let me describe to you my ideal client, what they often are saying when they need my services and how best to introduce them to me."

No conversation you have is ever going to fit neatly together as I have described above. You get to these questions over time and as the opportunity presents itself.

— ◆ —

Chapter 15:
Other Trends—The Demise of Big Law and Big Offices

◆

From Smaller Offices Local Firms Are Serving Bigger Clients

Your office is going to get smaller—it's going to be maybe half its current size—and your firm will be building a lot of small conference rooms. You'll also be eliminating secretarial stations the next time you move or when you remodel after the next renewal of your lease.

Those are some of the long term trends for the business of law revealed recently by a principal of Altman Weil at the Tennessee State Convention of the Association of Legal Administrators. I was there speaking about marketing, billing rates and the role of traditional relationships alongside social media and sat in on the presentation.

Altman principal Ward Bower told the audience in Nashville in 2014 that the total square feet per lawyer in an efficiently designed, cost-effective law office has shrunk to 400 from nearly twice that on average pre-Great Recession.

"Lawyer offices are now works spaces, not meeting spaces," he said. "Meetings, even between a firm's lawyers, are held in conference rooms and not in lawyer offices. You have a lot more conference rooms of all sizes."

There aren't secretarial stations across from each lawyer's office in the new economy's floor configuration either, Bower said.

Bower made his comments while explaining the "Golden Era of Big Law" will not return. For three years the legal market has not grown and total spending has been static at $250 million in domestic fees, he said. I have a take on that statistic. Spending at Big Law firms is flat because most every corporate legal department is finding less expensive, equally-credentialed lawyers in local and regional firms to do the work. We represent those firms and see work coming in to them from the Fortune 1000 every day. It's premium rate work for the local and regional firm and being billed at 25 percent (or less) per hour than what is charged by a national.

To increase profitability big law firms will continue to merge. These will mostly be acquisitions of firms of fewer than 25 lawyers by much larger firms seeking to create broader geographic footprints, Bower said.

How successful are such mergers? Of 117 mergers since 2002 an analysis by Altman showed 77 percent resulted in increased profitability in the first year. More than 90 percent had higher profits after five years when revenues were adjusted for inflation.

After saying that, Bower admitted the profitability jump hinges on the known phenomena that five percent of lawyers leave a firm they merge with after the first year. We all well know that after five years the percentage is far higher. I represent dozens of lawyers who merged into big firms and who within a few years have left and are recreating their former local firm—and gradually taking back clients of the firm into which they merged at lower rates.

Bower also said firms that can create a well understood and meaningful brand reported 10 percent greater profitability than firms that blended in with their competition. "You have to be known for something important to your client in a saturated market." he said. That's easy to say and much harder to do. So many branding initiatives produce meaningless taglines and imagery.

About Bob Weiss

Bob Weiss is considered one of the pioneers of law firm marketing, litigation publicity and public relations. Over the past 20+ years, he has written firm and practice group marketing plans, coached lawyers, developed law firm retreats, and conducted trainings, client interviews and surveys for local, regional and national firms.

His clients include firms involved in mass torts, catastrophic accident cases, corporate and transactional law and defense litigation. He also represents niche firms practicing domestic, election, criminal, immigration, insurance recovery and bad faith law.

His commentaries have appeared in the *ABA Journal, New Jersey Law Journal, Law Practice Magazine, Marketing for Lawyers, Attorney At Work* and *Lawyers Weekly* among other publications.

Major presentations he has made include addressing litigation publicity management, ethics, and extending the attorney-client privilege to talks with public relations personnel at the Annual Meeting of the American Bar Association, and presenting research on how to attract higher-value personal injury cases at the Annual Convention of the American Association for Justice. He has lectured on business development and ethics at meetings of domestic and international law firm networks and to numerous chapters of the Association of Legal Administrators.

His firm, Alyn-Weiss & Associates, publishes two respected and often-cited national marketing effectiveness surveys. One measures expenditures and identifies the most effective tactics employed by plaintiff practices. The other measures expenditures and identifies the most effective tactics employed by corporate/transactional and defense groups.

Weiss' "Monthly Marketing Brief"®, written by Bob, is a well-known column published for many years in *Law Practice Today*, the e-zine of the Law Practice Management Section of the ABA. It is now distributed online.

Bob has been professionally involved in many major news stories and resulting litigation. This includes representing interests and targets in public policy disputes, grand jury investigations, Wall Street Ponzi schemes, the Lehman Brothers bankruptcy, MBS litigation, JonBenet Ramsey murder, the Columbine High School massacre and several university athlete recruiting sex scandals. He began his career as a correspondent with United Press International and *TIME* magazine, was a staff reporter for the New York Times Newspaper Group's Lakeland, Florida, *Ledger* and Scripps Howard's *Rocky Mountain News*, Colorado's largest daily newspaper, covering politics, the courts, police, and city hall.

The award-winning marketing and business development programs Bob and his team have created have helped firms dramatically increase in size and profitability enter new markets and most importantly, allowed many lawyers to reposition themselves into new areas of practice, in the process rejuvenating their careers and passion for the law.

Bob frequently lectures at the national meetings of law firm networks, facilitates law firm retreats and provides in-firm group lawyer training. He coaches a select number of lawyers individually at any given time. Contact Bob at 303-298-1676 or by email at weiss@themarketinggurus.com to discuss how he can help your marketing efforts. ◆

Made in the USA
Middletown, DE
02 February 2023

23792154R00126